INTERSECTIONS
Education, Politics, Law, and Policy

MW01132181

# Proto-Fascism
# in America:
## Neoliberalism and the
## Demise of Democracy

Henry A. Giroux

Phi Delta Kappa Educational Foundation
Bloomington, Indiana U.S.A.

Cover design
Victoria Voelker


Series Editors
Donovan R. Walling
David M. Ruetschlin

Phi Delta Kappa Educational Foundation
408 North Union Street
Post Office Box 789
Bloomington, Indiana 47402-0789
U.S.A.


Printed in the United States of America


Library of Congress Control Number 2004092701
ISBN 0-87367-852-4

# Table of Contents

# Introduction

The United States now has more police, prisons, spies, weapons, and soldiers than at any other time in its history. This radical shift in the size, scope, and influence of the military can be seen, on the one hand, in the redistribution in domestic resources and government funding away from social programs and into military-oriented security measures at home and into war abroad. According to journalist George Monbiot, the U.S. federal government "is now spending as much on war as it is on education, public health, housing, employment, pensions, food aid and welfare put together."[1] The United States is being radically transformed into a national security state, increasingly put under the sway of the military-corporate-industrial-educational complex. The military logic of fear, surveillance, and control is permeating our public schools, universities, streets, popular culture, and criminal justice system.

Since the events of 9/11 and the wars in Afghanistan and Iraq, the military has assumed a privileged place in American society. President Bush not only celebrates the military presence in American culture, he cultivates it by going out of his way to give speeches at military facilities, to talk to military personnel, and to address veterans groups. He often wears a military uniform when speaking to "captive audiences at military bases, defense plants, and on aircraft carriers."[2] He also takes advantage of the campaign value of military culture by using military symbolism as a political prop in order to attract the widest possible media attention. One glaring instance occurred on 1 May 2003 when Bush landed in an aviator flight uniform on the *USS Abraham Lincoln* in the Pacific Ocean, where he officially proclaimed the end of the Iraqi war. There was also his trip to Baghdad in 2003 to spend Thanksgiving Day with the troops, an event that attracted worldwide media coverage. But Bush has done more than take advantage of the military as a campaign prop to sell his domestic and foreign policies. His administration and the Republican Party, which now controls all three branches of government, have developed a new, if not dangerous, "and unprecedented confluence of our democratic institutions and the military."[3]

Kevin Baker claims that the military "has become the most revered institution in the country."[4] Soon after the Iraqi war, a Gallup Poll reported that more than 76% of Americans "expressed 'a great deal' or 'quite a lot' of confidence in their nation's military." Among a poll of 1,200 students conducted by Harvard University, 75% believed that the military would "do the right thing" most of the time. In addition, the students "characterized themselves as hawks over doves by a ratio of two to one."[5]

As the military becomes more popular in American life, its underlying values, social relations, ideology, and hyper-masculine aesthetic begin to spread into other aspects of American culture. Citizens are recruited as foot soldiers in the war on terrorism, urged to spy on their neighbors, to watch for suspicious-looking people, and to supply data to the government. As permanent war becomes a staple of everyday life, flags increasingly appear on windows, lapels, cars, and everywhere else as a show of support for both the expanding interests of empire abroad and the increasing militarization of the culture and social order at home. Major universities more intensively court the military establishment for Defense Department grants and, in doing so, become less open to either academic subjects or programs that encourage rigorous debate, dialogue, and critical thinking. Public schools not only have more military recruiters, they also have more military personnel teaching in the classrooms. J.R.O.T.C. programs increasingly are a conventional part of the school day.

Under the No Child Left Behind Act, "schools risk losing all federal aid if they fail to provide military recruiters full access to their students; the aid is contingent with complying with federal law."[6] Schools once were viewed as democratic public spheres that would teach students how to resist the militarization of democratic life, or at least to learn the skills to peacefully engage domestic and international problems. Now they serve as recruiting stations for students to fight enemies at home and abroad.

Schools are one of the most serious public spheres to come under the influence of military culture and values. Tough love now translates into zero tolerance policies that turn public schools into prison-like institutions, and students' rights increasingly diminish under the onslaught of a military-like discipline. Students in many schools, especially those in poor urban areas, are routinely searched, frisked, subjected to involuntary drug tests, maced, and carted off to jail. Elissa Gootman in a report on schools in New York City claims, "In some places, schools are resorting to zero-tolerance policies that put students in handcuffs for dress code violations."[7]

As educators turn over their responsibility for school safety to the police, the new security culture in public schools has turned them into "learning prisons,"[8] most evident in the ways in which schools are being "reformed" through the addition of armed guards, barbed-wire security fences, and lock-down drills. Recently, in Goose Creek, South Carolina, police conducted an early morning drug-sweep at Stratford High School. When the police arrived, they drew guns on students, handcuffed them, and made them kneel facing the wall.[9] No drugs were found in the raid. Though this incident was aired on the national news, there were barely any protests from the public.

But children and schools are not the only victims of a growing militarization of American society. The civil rights of people of color and immigrants, especially Arabs and Muslims, are being violated, often resulting in imprisonment, deportation, or government harrassment. All of this is happening in the name of anti-terrorism laws that increasingly are being used by the Bush Administration to justify abusive military campaigns abroad and to stifle dissent at home. Measures to combat terrorism now are used by the government to support an arms budget that is larger than all of the other major industrialized countries combined. Similarly, as Jeremy Brecher points out, "the escalating rhetoric of the 'War against Terrorism' to the 'Axis of Evil' has provided a model for belligerence and potentially for nuclear conflict from India and Pakistan to Israel and Palestine. This militarization of conflict has been justified by the terroristic attacks against the United States, but, as a *New York Times* editorial pointed out, 'Bush is using the anti-terrorism campaign to disguise an ideological agenda that has nothing to do with domestic defense or battling terrorism abroad'."[10] What is in fact being labeled as a war against terrorism is beginning to look increasingly like a war waged by the Bush Administration against democracy itself.

# The War at Home and Abroad

Following the tragic events of 11 September 2001, the United States garnered the sympathy and respect of many nations all over the globe. The killing of 3,000 innocent people by terrorist thugs not only offered a vivid example of a grotesque assault on human life and human rights, but also underscored the vulnerability of one of the world's most powerful democracies. Tragedy was followed by myriad examples of human courage among many Americans; and, for a short time, a spirit of political resilience gave the federal government a renewed credibility. The controversial, if often politically brutalizing, former mayor of New York City, Rudolph Guiliani, exhibited a new-found leadership that made all the more visible the principles, values, and sense of compassion central to a vibrant democracy. At the same time, the international community rallied behind the United States, whose democracy appeared wounded but whose strength was revealed in its willingness to respond to an egregious act of terrorism with displays of compassion and national unity. *Le Monde*, the French newspaper, captured this sense of international solidarity and support when it proclaimed, "We Are All Americans."

But within two years, the cache of respect and regard that had been accorded the Bush Administration both at home and

abroad dwindled considerably as an increasing number of
nations and individuals came to regard the United States as a
major threat to world peace, if not to democracy itself. As
Senator Robert C. Byrd put it, "In some corners of the world,
including some corners of Europe and Great Britain, our
beloved nation is now viewed as the world bully."[11] The Bush
Administration's unilateral policy quickly turned America's
allies into some of its most severe critics. Even *New York Times*
columnist Thomas Friedman, no enemy of dominant power,
asserted that "Europeans have embraced President Bush's for-
mulation that an 'axis of evil' threatens world peace. There's
only one small problem. President Bush thinks that axis of evil
is Iran, Iraq, and North Korea, and the Europeans think it's
Donald Rumsfeld, Dick Cheney, and Condi Rice."[12]

The events of September 11 hastened a major shift not only
in domestic and foreign policy, but also "in our nation's self-
understanding. It became commonplace to refer to an 'American Empire' and to the United States as 'the world's only
superpower'."[13] Embracing a policy molded largely by fear
and bristling with partisan, right-wing ideological interests,
the Bush Administration took advantage of the tragedy of 9/11
by adopting and justifying a domestic and foreign policy that
blatantly privileged security over freedom, the rule of the market over social needs, and militarization over human rights and
social justice. Multilateralism in foreign affairs gave way to
reckless unilateralism and a gross disregard for international
law and was fueled by a foreign policy that defined itself
through the arrogance of unbridled power. Refusing to ratify a
number of landmark international agreements, such as the
Antiballistic Missile Treaty, the International Criminal Court,
and the Kyoto Protocol, the Bush Administration increasingly
displayed an "insulting arrogance toward the United Nations
in general, and individual members in particular."[14]

National security was now part of a larger policy in which the
United States has the right to use preventive military force "to
eliminate a perceived threat, even if invented or imagined."[15]

Senator Byrd described the unprecedented Bush doctrine of pre-emptive strike as a reckless policy that sets a dangerous precedent, undermines Congress' constitutional authority to declare war, and produces a "rising tide of anti-Americanism across the globe."[16] Global hegemony became synonymous with national security as official policy proclaimed that any challenge to United States power and supremacy would be blocked by military force.[17] After the attack on Afghanistan, Iraq was invaded by American forces; and that attack was justified through what later was proved to be a series of blatant and misleading arguments by the Bush Administration.[18] Moreover, far from making the country safer, many foreign policy analysts, including Gareth Evans, former Australian foreign minister, argued that the invasion of Iraq served only to mobilize many in the Arab world into believing that the United States was more intent on humiliating the Islamic world than in bringing "democracy" to Iraq. Such actions on the part of the Bush Administration not only unified Islamic terrorists but also created a greater threat to Americans at home and abroad, but especially to those soldiers and personnel serving in Iraq and Afghanistan. As Evans puts it, "The unhappy truth is that the net result of the war on terror, so far at least, has been more war and more terror."[19]

What has become clear since the invasion of Iraq is the willingness of the Bush Administration to wage a war on terrorism at the expense of civil liberties, just as it scrapped a foreign policy that at least made a gesture toward democratic values for one that unleashes untold violence in the name of combating evil and exercising control over all other global powers. As Robert Jay Lifton points out, war has taken on a mythic and heroic status under the Bush Administration, "carried out for the defense of one's nation, to sustain its special historical destiny and the immortality of its people."[20] The real cost of such a doctrine is far from heroic, not only resulting in widespread fear, anxiety, massive suffering, and death, but also completely undermining the credibility of the American government as a bastion of democracy. Benjamin Barber puts the issue succinctly:

> It is hard for the U.S. to be the beacon of freedom that Bush's speech[es] celebrate — and the world so admires — when it has in many places come to be seen as the maker of war the world most fears. It is hard to lead a global struggle for human rights when the U.S. holds enemy aliens prisoners without rights and when Americans who criticize the preventive-war policy are vilified.[21]

On the domestic front, a strange mixture of neo-conservatives ideologues, free-market right-wingers, and evangelical Christians began to wage another kind of war not only against the social contract that had been put in place by Franklin Delano Roosevelt's New Deal and Lyndon Johnson's Great Society, but also against the secular government and the long-standing division between church and state, secular reason and religious beliefs. The needs of poor, working-class, and middle-class Americans are now under siege by the federal government, which instituted tax cuts for the richest 1%, increased corporate welfare, bankrolled a massive military machine, and turned a 2001 government surplus of $127 billion into a deficit of $455 billion by 2003.[22] In short, public assets have been hijacked by those at the top of the economic pyramid, leaving few public resources for financially strapped state and local governments to use for addressing new problems or long-term improvements.

One specific — and intended — outcome of this policy is that there is very little money or assistance available for those Americans most in need. The rich get tax handouts and corporate relief while the most basic healthcare services for children, the elderly, and the disabled are either cut or dramatically reduced.[23] For example, "about 270,000 children of low-income, working parents have been barred from health insurance programs in the nine states where estimates are available."[24] The Center on Budget and Policy Priorities reports that with 34 states making cuts over the last two years in public health insurance programs, "Some 1.2 million to 1.6 million low-income people — including 490,000 to 650,000 children and large numbers of parents, seniors, and people with disabilities — have lost public funded health coverage as a result."[25] More than 37% of all children lack health insurance in the world's wealthiest nation. Under President Bush's 2004 budget, it has been estimated that about "600,000 children will lose child care and after school services."[26]

The long-standing social contract that was central to American democracy is not simply deteriorating, it is under sustained attack by free-market extremists and right-wingers. In what is truly one of the most glaring contradictions of the current Republican-led government, vast numbers of people are now cut from the most basic social provisions and public resources at the same time that Bush and his aids increasingly are using the hyped-up language of religious morality and "compassionate conservatism" to defend the discourse of free-market fundamentalism and a politics that largely caters to the rich and powerful. Congressman Bernie Sanders, in an exchange with FED Chairman Alan Greenspan, provides a more specific indication of the social costs incurred by neo-conservative and right-wing free-market policies recently put into place:

> You [Greenspan] talk about an improving economy while we have lost 3 million private sector jobs in the last two years, long-term unemployment is more than tripled, unemployment is higher than it's been since 1994. We have a $4 trillion national debt, 1.3 million Americans have lost their health insurance, millions of seniors can't afford prescription drugs, middle-class families can't send their kids to college because they don't have the money to do that, bankruptcy cases have increased by a record-breaking 23 percent, business investment is at its lowest level in more than 50 years, CEOs make more than 500 times what their workers make, the middle class is shrinking, we have the greatest gap

between the rich and the poor of any industrialized
nation, and this is an economy that is improving?[27]

President George W. Bush sees no irony in proclaiming in
one speech after another, largely to highly selected groups of
conservatives, that he is a "born again" Christian, all the while
ruthlessly passing legislation that weakens such environmental
laws as the Clean Air Act, opposing a United Nations resolu-
tion to fund global AIDS education and prevention, undermining the stability of Medicare, waging a budget war against
disadvantaged children, denying millions of poor working
adults a child tax credit, squandering the federal surplus on tax
cuts for the rich, and increasing corporate welfare to the tune
of $125 billion as he decreases social benefits for millions of
Americans, especially those who are poverty stricken, old,
young, and disabled.[28]

Religious fundamentalism appears to be growing in the
United States, and the movement has received an enormous
boost from those in power who think of themselves as
"chosen." At the same time, this mounting religious fervor,
with its Manichean division of the world into the modalities
of good and evil, remains inhospitable to dissent and reinforces a distinctly undemocratic view of patriotism. The slide
into self-righteousness and intolerance appears to be on the
rise in American life as politicians and moralists lay claim to
an alleged monopoly on the truth, based on their religious
conviction — an outlandish presumption matched only by an
utter disdain for those who do not share their worldview.[29]
Under the Bush Administration, patriotism is now legitimated
through the physics of unaccountable power and unquestioned authority, defined crudely in the dictum, "Either you
are with us or with the terrorists."[30] When millions all over the
world protested the U.S. invasion of Iraq, not to mention the
protests of numerous international allies, Bush and his evangelical counselors simply dismissed such criticism as evidence
of weakness and a refusal to acknowledge evil. As Gary Wills

sums up: "Question the policy, and you no longer believe in evil — which is the same, in this context, as not believing in God. That is the religious test on which our president is grading us."[31]

This culture of intolerance and patriotic jingoism are readily shared and legitimated by the corporate-controlled media and an army of intellectual cheerleaders, largely bankrolled by a powerful conservative money-machine including the Olin, Heritage, Coors, and Scaife Family Foundations. Such absolutes, of course, have little respect for difference, dissent, or even democracy itself. Politics in this instance has much less in common with public engagement, dialogue, and democratic governance than with a heavy reliance on institutions that rule through fear and, if necessary, brute force. Right-wing media favorite Ann Coulter not only asserts in her book, *Treason*, that "liberals are either traitors or idiots,"[32] but argues elsewhere that John Walker, the young American captured in Afghanistan, should be given the death penalty "in order to physically intimidate liberals, by making them realize that they can be killed too. Otherwise they can be turned into outright traitors."[33] Inspired by the media success, the former campus activist Jack Abramoff, once former national chair of the College Republicans, unveiled the organization's master plan in the following anti-democratic terms: "We are not just trying to win the next election. We're winning the next generation. . . . It's not our job to seek peaceful co-existence with the left. Our job is to remove them from power permanently."[34] And further, Kathleen Parker, a conservative columnist, published an article in which she cites, without challenge, a quote from "a friend" who suggested that a number of Democratic Party candidates "should be lined up and shot."[35]

Such rhetorical interventions are about more than eliminating the critical function of dissent or thinking itself — both vital to the democratic health of a society — they embody a kind of violence that suggests that critics should be targeted and punished. This type of polemic is characteristic of a distrust of the intellectual world and a deep-seated rejection of Enlightenment thought as the "beginning of modern depravity."[36] Moreover, this "disagreement is treason" bravado has a lot in common with traditional fascist movements that attacked critical thinking as a way of "exploiting and exacerbating the natural fear of difference."[37] Such rhetorical interventions are about more than eliminating the critical function of dissent or thinking itself — both vital to the democratic health of a society — they embody a kind of symbolic violence reminiscent of a totalitarian ideology in which the suggestion that critics should be targeted and punished became a gruesome reality. Put differently, the embrace of anti-intellectualism and distrust of critical thought and intellectuals supports authoritarianism over and against democracy.

Such rhetoric cannot be dismissed as an aberration. Unfortunately, this kind of extreme language is found not only among eccentric right-wing intellectuals; it also is on prominent display in mainstream Republican Party rhetoric. For example, when the Republican Party launched its 2004 campaign to re-elect George W. Bush, it produced an ad that stated, "Some are now attacking the president for attacking the terrorists." As rhetorically dishonest as it is opportunistic, the ad both misrepresents the complexity of a post-9/11 world and suggests that critics of Bush's policies support terrorism. Critics are not supporting terrorism. Instead, they are pointing out that the Bush Administration has squandered much-needed funds by invading Iraq and, in doing so, has lost sight of the real threats posed by terrorists while seriously "undermining the campaign against terrorism."[38]

I am not suggesting that all conservatives support this kind of sophistry or believe in these deeply undemocratic sentiments and actions. But I do think the right-wing takeover of the Republican Party and its relentless appeal to the moral high ground — coupled with its ongoing demonization and punishment of those on the right and left who dare to question its policies — shut down the possibility for dialogue and exchange, thereby silencing those who wish to make power visible, as well as politically and morally accountable, in a democracy. But this type of politics does more than celebrate its own intolerance, it also lays the groundwork for a kind of authoritarianism that views democracy as both a burden and a threat.

As the federal government is restructured under the Bush Administration, it relies more heavily on its militarizing functions, gives free reign to the principle of security at the expense of public service, and endorses property rights over human rights. As a consequence, democracy is imperiled as the emerging security state offers the American people the false choice between being safe or free.[39] In the name of security, the distinction between government power and "laws governing the rights of people accused of a crime"[40] is lost. A web of secrecy has emerged under the Bush Administration that gives it the opportunity to abuse democratic freedoms and, at the same time, to make itself unaccountable for its actions by using national security to its legal advantage. Under the veil of legislated secrecy, the U.S. government now can name individuals as terrorists without offering them a public hearing and break into private homes and tap the phones of U.S. citizens without a warrant. As if this were not bad enough, constitutional freedoms and civil liberties are further compromised by the power of government agents to subpoena anybody's telephone, medical, bookstore, library, or university records "simply by certifying that the records are needed for an investigation of international terrorism."[41] The CIA and Pentagon are allowed to engage in domestic intelligence work, and the USA Patriot Act allows people to be detained secretly and indefinitely without access to either lawyers or a jury trial.[42] Even children as young as 14 have been held without legal representation as enemy combatants in possibly inhumane conditions at the military's infamous Camp Delta at Guantanamo Bay, Cuba, along with more than 600 "enemy combatants" who still are being detained. Under such cir-

cumstances, as Arundhati Roy argues, "the fundamental governing principles of democracy are not just being subverted
but deliberately sabotaged. This kind of democracy is the
problem, not the solution."[43] Dissent does not come easy in a
country where people can be detained, deported, tried without representation, and held indefinitely in a jail under a legal
policy of enforced secrecy.

One recent example can be found in willingness of the government to serve subpoenas to four activists who attended an
anti-war conference at Drake University on 15 November 2003.
Not only were the students ordered to appear before a grand
jury investigation, but Drake University was ordered by a federal judge to provide information about the anti-war conference, specifically records of those who were in control of the
conference and those who attended.[44] In this instance, there is
strong evidence to suggest that the USA Patriot Act is being
used to target certain forms of political activities, intimidate
protesters, and stifle the free speech rights of those protesting
the policies of the Bush Administration.[45]

Authoritarianism's shadow becomes increasingly darker as
society is organized relentlessly around a culture of unquestioned obedience, fear, cynicism, and unbridled self-interest
— a society in which the government promotes legislation
urging neighbors to spy on each other and the President
endorses a notion of patriotism based on moral absolutes and
an alleged Christian mandate to govern (with a little help, of
course, from Jeb Bush and the U.S. Supreme Court).[46] The
arrogance of power is on full display as both the President and
the attorney general, in the name of national security, have
refused to give congressional committees information they
have requested about a range of government actions, including Vice President Cheney's meetings in the White House
with representatives of the energy industry and materials
related to the government's anti-terrorist policies prior to the
tragic events of 9/11.

# Proto-Fascism and the Rhetoric Against Extremism

It is against the restructuring of American power and ideology that a number of critics at home and across the globe have begun to suggest that a new form of political tyranny is emerging in the United States, one that threatens not only its underlying democratic values but also peace abroad.[47] The chorus of complaints and criticisms is disturbing. One of the world's most respected elder statesman, South African leader Nelson Mandela, claimed in an interview with *Newsweek* that George W. Bush's rhetoric about democracy is a sham and that U.S foreign policy is motivated by a "desire to please the arms and oil industries in the United States." He further argued that a foreign policy built on the unilateral right to invade alleged enemies both undermines the United Nations and sets a dangerous standard in foreign affairs for the enemies of democracy. In light of the United States invasion of Iraq, Mandela insisted that "the United States has become a threat to world peace."[48] He is not alone in thinking this. In a survey of 7,500 Europeans, the United States was ranked second, above even Kim Jong Il's nuclear-armed North Korea and terrorist-sponsoring Iran, as the greatest threat to world peace.[49] Ken Livingston, the mayor of London, denounced

George W. Bush as "the greatest threat to life on this planet that we've most probably ever seen."[50]

An equally disturbing critique has emerged suggesting that the United States government not only poses a danger to world peace, but also has completely abdicated its democratic traditions — and its "conserving" values — in favor of radical extremism. As George Soros, respected philanthropist and multibillionaire, puts it, "The Republican Party has been captured by a bunch of extremists."[51] U.S. Senator Robert Byrd on the floor of Congress in October 2003 went so far as to compare Bush's use of the media to the propaganda techniques employed by the leaders of the Third Reich. Drawing comparisons between the Bush Administration and the infamous Nazi murderer, Herman Goering, Byrd offered a biting criticism of the growing extremism in the Bush Administration.[52] In his book, *Made in Texas*, Michael Lind argues that Bush is one of the worst presidents in American history and that his mission is to carry out the economic and foreign policy agenda of the far right.[53] The notion of extremism also has been raised by former national security advisor to President Jimmy Carter, Zbiginiew Brzezinski, who claims that the Bush Administration's "war on terrorism" represents "a rather narrow and extremist vision of foreign policy of the world's primary superpower."[54] Administration insiders, such as Karen Kwiatowski, a former Air Force lieutenant and specialist in the office of the Undersecretary of Defense for Policy, claims that "the country has been hijacked" by neoconservatives who are running a shadow government.[55] And in response to Bush's radical market fundamentalism and neoliberal ideology — with its belief that the market should be the organizing principle for all political, social, and economic decisions — American Nobel Prize laureate for economics George A. Akerlof stated in an interview with *Der Spiegel* magazine that:

> this is the worst government the US has ever had in its more than 200 years of history. It has engaged in extra-

ordinarily irresponsible policies not only in foreign and
economic but also in social and environmental policy.
This is not normal government policy. Now is the time
for people to engage in civil disobedience.[56]

An even more serious attack against the Bush Administration has emerged among a number of critics who claim that
the United States is increasingly abandoning democracy and
descending into the icy political waters of a new form of
authoritarianism. Two critics who have received some attention in the popular press for such arguments are Arundhati
Roy, the Indian novelist and social activist, and Sheldon Wolin,
an emeritus professor of politics at Princeton University. Both
individuals have argued that the specter of a creeping fascism
is becoming a reality in the United States and that democracy
is not just challenged but transformed by a form of authoritarianism that is shaping political culture and daily life almost
unnoticed. For Roy, the commanding institutions of American life have now been sold to the highest bidder, largely subverted by neoliberal capitalists who have "mastered the tech-
nique of infiltrating the instruments of democracy — the
'independent' judiciary, the 'free' press . . . and molding them
to their purpose."[57] Roy is particularly concerned about the
corporate control of the media in the United States and the
role it plays in perpetuating an ultra-patriotic fervor that shuts
down dissent and renders dominant power free from responsibility for its actions. She points in particular to Clear Channel Communications, the largest radio broadcaster in the
United States, reaching more than 200 million people, and
the role it has played in organizing pro-war rallies, refusing to
play artists critical of the war, and engaging in ongoing efforts
to manufacture not only consent but also the news itself.[58]
Citing how democracy is undermined by the commercialization of public space, the control of the media, the ongoing
erosion of civil liberties, the rise of repressive state power, and
the emergence of an era of systematic automated surveillance

— all of which is reinforced by the alleged war against terrorism — Roy argues that the price of alleged new democracy in Iraq and other countries is the "death of real democracy at home."[59] In light of these dramatic shifts away from democratic principles and social relations, she argues that American society has entered a historic period when dominant economic and state power has removed itself from the dynamics of political constraint and public accountability. The overall result is that the space of freedom is undermined, constituting a step toward fascism. She writes:

> The incipient, creeping fascism of the past few years has been groomed by many of our "democratic" institutions. Everyone has flirted with it — [Congress], the press, the police, the administration, the public. Even "secularists" have been guilty of helping to create the right climate. Each time you defend the right of an institution, any institution (including the Supreme Court), to exercise unfettered, unaccountable power that must never be challenged, you move toward fascism. To be fair, perhaps not everyone recognized the early signs for what they were.[60]

Roy was criticized heavily in the American media for opposing the war in Iraq, the implication being that such criticism amounted to supporting terrorism, a position legitimated in the highest reaches of the government of the United States and stated publicly by Attorney General John Ashcroft[61] — a charge I've already established as routine. She also was condemned roundly for suggesting that the United States was increasingly behaving like a fascist state.[62] Roy's use of the term "fascism" was intended not so much to imply a crude parallel between the Bush Administration and Hitler's Nazi Germany as it was to suggest how extremist the Republican Party has become since the appointment of George W. Bush in 2000.

Sheldon Wolin, a world-renowned political theorist, wrote a much more damning article about the growing authoritarianism in the United States. Refusing to engage in rhetorical excesses, Wolin argues that "we are facing forms of domination that exceed the old vocabulary and so we have to try to find language that corresponds to this condition."[63] Rather than argue that the United States has become an authoritarian regime in the manner of Nazi Germany or fascist Italy during the 1930s and 1940s, Wolin, like Roy, argues that the United States exhibits both similarities with and differences from these regimes. Specifically, the United States shares with both of these totalitarian societies an administration and political party whose aim is "to promote empire abroad and corporate [interests] at home," while at the same time "seeking total power."[64] Wolin argues that the Bush Administration is moving toward an "inverted totalitarianism," in sharing the Nazi "aspiration toward unlimited power and aggressive expansionism, their methods and actions seem upside down."[65] Whereas the Nazis filled the streets with thugs in their drive toward unlimited power, the Bush Administration centers its power in the unbridled reach of government and the massively concentrated power of a corporate-controlled media. And whereas the Nazis subordinated big business to the political regime, under the Bush regime corporate power shapes political policy. In addition, "while Nazi totalitarianism strove to give the masses a sense of collective power and strength, *Kraft durch Freude* ('Strength Through Joy'), inverted totalitarianism promotes a sense of weakness, of collective futility."[66] For Wolin, these differences suggest a departure in the way political power is mobilized and a reconfiguration of the institutional and social agents at the heart of such a struggle. But in both cases the aim is the same: the elimination of democracy and the concentration of power and control in the hands of a single party and the ruling corporate elite. According to Wolin, all of the elements are in place for what he calls the "attempted transformation of a tolerably free society into a variant of the extreme regimes of the past century." He writes:

Thus the elements are in place: a weak legislative body, a legal system that is both compliant and repressive, a party system in which one party, whether in opposition or in the minority, is bent upon reconstituting the existing system so as to permanently favor a ruling class of the wealthy, the well-connected and the corporate, while leaving the poorer citizens with a sense of helplessness and political despair, and, at the same time, keeping the middle classes dangling between fear of unemployment and expectations of fantastic rewards once the new economy recovers. That scheme is abetted by a sycophantic and increasingly concentrated media; by the integration of universities with their corporate benefactors; by a propaganda machine institutionalized in well-funded think tanks and conservative foundations; by the increasingly closer cooperation between local police and national law enforcement agencies aimed at identifying terrorists, suspicious aliens and domestic dissidents.[67]

The most public rebuke to Wolin came from James Traub writing in the *New York Times Magazine*. Traub denounced critics such as Roy and Wolin as "Weimar Whiners" and argued that any comparison between the Bush Administration and the Hitler regime "constitutes a gross trivialization of the worst event in modern history."[68] According to Traub, fascism is a term that was abused by the left in the 1960s and is being used recklessly once again by those criticizing the Bush regime. His argument suggests that fascism is a historically specific movement whose ideology cannot be applied outside of the conditions in which it emerged. In short, Traub implies that any suggestion that the United States is becoming a fascist state is simply preposterous. Perfectly at ease with the increasing repressions established under the Bush Administration, as well as the violations of civil liberties put into place by John Ashcroft, Traub cites Norman Siegel, the former head of the New York Civil Liberties Union, to suggest that the USA Patriot Act has nothing to do with a creeping fascism and may be well-justified as part of the current war on terrorism. If Traub is to be believed, democracy in the United States is as strong as ever.

However, Traub's argument is informed by the mistaken notion that the collapse of fascist regimes after World War II represented the demise of fascism. What Traub ignores is the distinction between the state-sponsored regime and the ideology and movement. No critic is saying that the United States now mimics the fascism of the 1930s; rather, the point is that it appears to be developing a number of characteristics that are endemic to fascist ideology. Traub has no sense of different degrees or gradations of authoritarianism, of fascism as an ideology that can reconstitute itself in different ideas, practices, and arguments. Instead, he clings to both a reductive understanding of fascism and a simplistic binary logic that holds that a country is either authoritarian or democratic. He has no language for entertaining either a mixture of both systems or a degree of unaccountable power that might suggest a more updated, if not different, form of authoritarianism.

# Authoritarianism and Proto-Fascism in the United States

Fascism and authoritarianism are important categories that need to be mined in order to explore the changing nature of power, control, and rule in the United States and the challenge that such changes pose to a democracy clearly under siege. I want to make clear from the outset that I am not suggesting the United States is engaged in a process of genocidal terror against racialized populations — though the increase in police brutality in the last decade against people of color, coupled with the rise of a prison-industrial-military complex that primarily punishes black men, cannot be overlooked.[69] Nor can the increased attack by the American government on the rights of many innocent Arabs, Muslims, and immigrants be understood as anything other than a kind of totalitarian time-warp in which airport terminals now resemble state prisons as foreign nationals are fingerprinted, photographed, and interrogated.[70] Rather, I am arguing that the United States has many earmarks of a growing authoritarianism.

Fascism is not an ideological apparatus frozen in a particular historical period, but a theoretical and political signpost for understanding how democracy can be subverted, if not destroyed. In the 1980s Bertram Gross wrote *Friendly Fascism,* in which he argued that if fascism came to the United States, it would not embody the fascist characteristics that were associated with its legacies in the past.[71] There would be no Nuremberg rallies, doctrines of racial superiority, government-sanctioned book burnings, death camps, or the abrogation of the constitution. In short, fascism would not take the form of an ideological grid from the past simply downloaded onto another country under different historical conditions. On the contrary, he believed that fascism is an eternal danger and has the ability to become relevant under new conditions taking on familiar forms of thought that resonate with nativist traditions, experiences, and political relations. Umberto Eco in his discussion of "Eternal Fascism" argues that any updated version of fascism will not openly assume the mantle of historical fascism; rather, new forms of authoritarianism will appropriate some of its elements. Like Gross, Eco argues that fascism, if it comes to America, will have a different guise, though it will be no less destructive of democracy. He writes:

> Ur-Fascism [a term meaning Eternal Fascism] is still around us, sometimes in plainclothes. It would be much easier for us if there appeared on the world scene somebody saying, "I want to reopen Auschwitz, I want the Blackshirts to parade again in the Italian squares." Life is not that simple. Ur-Fascism can come back under the most innocent of disguises. Our duty is to uncover it and to point our finger at any of its new instances — everyday, in every part of the world. Franklin Roosevelt's words of November 4, 1938, are worth recalling: "If American democracy ceases to move forward as a living force, seeking day and night by peaceful means to better the lot of our citizens, fascism will grow in strength in our land." Freedom and liberation are an unending task.[72]

In order to make a distinction between the old and new forms of fascism, I want to use the term *proto-fascism* not only because it suggests a different constellation of elements and forms pointing toward its reconstitution, but also because it has "the beauty of familiarity, and rightly in many cases reveals a deliberate attempt to make fascism relevant in new conditions."[73] The point here is not to obscure the distinctiveness of the old fascism but to highlight how some of its central elements are emerging in contemporary forms.

Precise accounts of the meaning of fascism abound, and I have no desire, given its shifting nature, to impose a rigid definition with universal pretensions. But most scholars agree that fascism is a mass movement that emerges out of a failed democracy and that its ideology is extremely anti-liberal, anti-democratic, and anti-socialistic. It also is marked by an "elaborate ideology which covers all aspects of man's existence and which contains a powerful chiliastic [messianic or religious] moment."[74] As a political philosophy, fascism exalts the nation and race — or some purified form of national identity — over the individual, supports centralized dictatorial power, demands blind obedience from the masses, and promotes a top-down revolution. As a social order, it generally is characterized by: a system of terror directed against perceived enemies of the state, a monopolistic control of the mass media, an expanding prison system, a state monopoly of weapons, the existence of privileged groups and classes, control of the economy by a limited number of people, unbridled corporatism, "the appeal to emotion and myth rather than reason, the glorification of violence on behalf of a national cause; the mobilization and militarization of civil society; [and] an expansionist foreign policy intended to promote national greatness."[75]

I argue in this essay that the specter of fascism resides in the lived relations of a given social order and the ways in which such relations exacerbate the material conditions of inequality, undercut a sense of individual and social agency, hijack democratic values, and promote a deep sense of hopelessness and cynicism. Proto-fascism as both an ideology and a set of social practices emerges within the lived contradictions that mark such relations, scorning the present while calling for a revolution that rescues a deeply anti-modernist past as a way to revolutionize the future. Mark Neocleous touches on the anti-modernist nature of fascist ideology in his discussion of a "reactionary modernism" that is typical of the New Right and whose project is essentially ultraconservative. He writes:

> [The New Right] pitted itself against the existing order — the post-war "consensus" regarding welfarism and the quasi corporate management of capitalism — in the light of an image of past national glory (a mythic and contradictory image, but no less powerful for that). The central elements of New Right politics — an aggressive leadership, uncompromising stance on law and order, illiberal attitude on moral questions generally and certain political questions such as race and immigration, an attack on the labor movement and a defense of private property, and a forthright nationalism — all combine in a politics of reaction: a reassertion of the principle of private property and capital accumulation as the *raison d'être* of modern society, alongside an authoritarian moralism requiring excessive state power as a means of policing civil society. If there is such a thing as the New Right distinct from "traditional" conservatism, then it lies in its being a reactionary modernism of our times.[76]

The emerging proto-fascism that threatens American democracy can best be understood by examining a number of characteristics that relate it to both an older form of fascism and a set of contemporary conditions that give it a distinctive character. After documenting and analyzing these central, though far from exhaustive, features of proto-fascism, I want to conclude by examining how neoliberalism provides a unique set of conditions for both producing and legitimating the central tendencies of proto-fascism.

The cult of traditionalism and a reactionary modernism are central features of proto-fascism and are alive and well in Bush's America. The alliance of neoconservatives, extremist evangelical Christians, and free-market advocates on the political Right imagines a social order modeled on the presidency of William McKinley and the values of the robber barons. The McKinley presidency lasted from 1897 to 1901 and "had a consummate passion to serve corporate and imperial power."[77] This was an age when blacks, women, immigrants, and minorities of class "knew their place"; big government served the exclusive interests of the corporate monopolists; commanding institutions were under the sway of narrow political interests; welfare was a private enterprise; and labor unions were kept in place by the repressive forces of the state. All of these conditions are being reproduced under the leadership of an extremist element of the Republican Party that holds sway over all branches of government. William Greider, writing in *The Nation*, comments on the cult of traditionalism and anti-modernism that characterizes this administration and its return to a past largely defined through egregious inequality,[78] corporate greed, hyper-commercialism, political corruption, and an utter disdain for economic and political democracy. According to Greider, the overall ambition of the Bush Administration and his right-wing allies is:

> to roll back the twentieth century, quite literally. That is, defenestrate the federal government and reduce its scale and powers to a level well below what it was before the New Deal's centralization. With that accomplished, movement conservatives envision a restored society in which the prevailing values and power relationships resemble the America that existed around 1900, when William McKinley was President. . . . [Under such circumstances] governing authority and resources are dispersed from Washington, returned to local levels and also to individuals and private institutions, most notably corporations and religious organizations. The primacy of private property rights is re-established over the shared public priorities expressed in government regulation. Above all, private wealth — both enterprises and individuals with higher incomes — are permanently insulated

from the progressive claims of the graduated income tax.[79]

A second feature connecting the old fascism to its updated version is the ongoing corporatization of civil society and the diminishing of public space. The latter refers to the fact that corporate space is destroying democratic public spheres, eliminating those public spaces where norm-establishing communication takes place. Viewed primarily as an economic investment rather than as a central democratic sphere for fostering the citizen-based processes of deliberation, debate, and dialogue, public space is being consistently diminished through the relentless dynamic of privatization and commercialization. The important notion that space can be used to cultivate citizenship is now transformed by a new "common sense" that links it almost entirely to the production of consumers. The inevitable correlate to this logic is that providing space for democracy to grow is no longer a priority. As such theorists as Jurgen Habermas and David Harvey have argued, the space of critical citizenship cannot flourish without the reality of public space.[80] Put differently, "the space of citizenship is as important as the idea of citizenship."[81] As a political category, space is crucial to any critical understanding of how power circulates, how disciplinary practices are constructed, and how social control is organized. But, as Margaret Kohn points out in her landmark study on radical space, "spatial practices can also contribute to transformative politics."[82] Moreover, space as a political category performs invaluable theoretical work in connecting material struggles to ideas, theories to concrete practices, and the places where politics operates to the concerns of everyday life. Without public space, it becomes more difficult for individuals to imagine themselves as political agents or to understand the necessity for developing a discourse capable of defending civic institutions. Public space confirms the idea of individuals and groups having a public voice, thus drawing a distinction between civic liberty and market liberty.

The demands of citizenship affirm the social as a political concept in opposition to it being understood as simply an economic category; the sanctity of the town hall or public square in American life is grounded in the crucial recognition that citizenship has to be cultivated in noncommercialized spaces. Indeed, democracy itself needs public spheres where education as a condition for democracy can flourish, where people can meet and where democratic identities, values, and relations have the time "to grow and flourish."[83] Zygmunt Bauman captures the historical importance of public spaces for nourishing civic discourses and engaging citizens, as well as the ethical consequences of the current disappearances of noncommodified spheres. He writes:

> These meeting places . . . public spaces — agoras and forums in their various manifestations, places where agendas are set, private affairs are made public . . . were also the sites in which *norms were created* — so that justice could be done, and apportioned horizontally, thus re-forging the conversationalists into a *community*, set apart and integrated by the shared criteria of evaluation. Hence a territory stripped of public space provides little chance for norms being debated, for values to be confronted, to clash and to be negotiated. The verdicts of right and wrong, beauty and ugliness, proper and improper, useful and useless may only descend from on high, from regions never to be penetrated by any but a most inquisitive eye; the verdicts are unquestionable since no questions may be meaningfully addressed to the judges and since the judges left no address — not even an e-mail address — and no one can be sued where they reside. No room is left for the "local opinion leaders"; no room is left for the "local opinion" as such.[84]

A third feature of the emerging proto-fascism is the relationship between the constructions of an ongoing culture of fear and a form of patriotic correctness designed to bolster a rampant nationalism and a selective popularism. Fear is mobilized through both the war on terrorism and "the sovereign pronouncement of a 'state of emergency' [which] generates a wild zone of power, barbaric and violent operating without democratic oversight in order to combat an 'enemy' that threatens the existence of not merely and not mainly its citizens, but its sovereignty."[85] As Stanley Aronowitz points out, the national security state is now organized through "a combination of internal terrorism and the threat of external terrorism," which reinforces "its most repressive functions."[86]

The threat of outside terrorism redefines the rules of war since there is no traditional state or enemy to fight. One consequence is that all citizens and noncitizens are viewed as potential terrorists and must prove their innocence through either consent or complicity with the national security state. Under such circumstances, patriotic fervor marks the line between terrorist and nonterrorists. Jingoistic patriotism is now mobilized in the highest reaches of government, in the media, and throughout society; put on perpetual display through the rhetoric of celebrities, journalists, and nightly television news anchors; and relentlessly buttressed by the never-ending waving of flags — on cars, trucks, clothes, houses, and the lapels of TV anchors — as well as through the use of mottoes, slogans, and songs. As a rhetorical ploy to silence dissent, patriotism is used to name as unpatriotic any attempt to either make governmental power and authority responsive to its consequences at home or to question how the appeal to nationalism is being used to legitimate the government's bad-faith aspirations to empire building overseas. As I mentioned earlier, this type of anti-liberal thinking is deeply distrustful of critical inquiry, mistakes dissent for treason, constructs politics on the moral absolutes of "us and them," and views difference and democracy as threats to consensus and national identity. Such patriotic fervor fuels a system of militarized control that not only repudiates the authority of international law, but also relies on a notion of preventive war in order to project the fantasies of unbridled American power all over the globe. Richard Falk argues that it is precisely this style of imperial control — fed by the desire for incontestable military preeminence in the world — and the use of authoritarian modes of regulation by the state at home that have given rise to what he describes as the threat of global fascism posed by the current administration. He writes:

> But why fascist? . . . First of all, the combination of unchallengeable military preeminence with a rejection by the US government of the restraining impact of international law and the United Nations. . . . Secondly, the US government in moving against terrorism has claimed sweeping power to deal with the concealed Al Qaeda network. . . . the character of the powers claimed include secret detentions, the authority to designate American citizens as "enemy combatants" without any rights, the public consideration of torture as a permissible police practice in anti-terrorist work, the scrutiny applied to those of Muslim faith, the reliance on assassination directed at terrorist suspects wherever they are found, and numerous invasions of privacy directed at ordinary people. . . . The slide toward fascism at home is given tangible expression by these practices, but it is also furthered by an uncritical and chauvinistic patriotism, by the release of periodic alarmist warnings of mega-terrorist imminent attacks that fail to materialize, and by an Attorney General, John Ashcroft, who seems to exult in the authoritarian approach to law enforcement.[87]

A fourth feature of proto-fascism is the attempt to control the mass media through government regulation, consolidated corporate ownership, or sympathetic media moguls and spokespeople. The use of government regulation is evident in the Bush-appointed FCC's attempts to pass legislation favoring media monopolies that would undermine opposition and organize consent through a "capillary network of associations with vast powers of social and cultural persuasion."[88] Indeed, media regulation has promoted, rather than limited, the con-

solidation of media ownership in the United States. As a powerful form of public pedagogy, the media set the agenda for what
information is included or excluded. They provide the narratives for understanding the past and present; distinguish
between high- and low-status knowledge; provide subject
positions; legitimate particular values; and have the power to
deeply influence how people define the future. The media do
not merely manufacture consent; they go so far as to produce
the news and offer up the knowledge, skills, and values
through which citizenship is lived and democracy defined. In
the process, the media have assumed a major role in providing
the conditions necessary for creating knowledgeable citizens
capable of participating fully in shaping and governing society
by having access to a wide range of knowledge and information. At the risk of exaggerating this issue, I must stress that in
the 21st century the media, as well as the culture they produce, distribute, and sanction, have become the most important educational force in creating citizens and social agents
capable of putting existing institutions into question and
making democracy work — or doing just the opposite.

Unfortunately, the power of the media, along with the
agenda they set, is now in the hands of a limited number of
transnational corporations; and the number of owners is getting smaller. Robert McChesney and John Nichols argue that
"the U.S. media system is dominated by about ten transnational conglomerates including Disney, AOL TimeWarner,
News Corporation, Viacom, Vivendi Universal, Sony, Liberty, Bertelsmann, AT&T Comcast, and General Electric
(NBC)."[89] Before the Telecommunications Act of 1996, a single firm could own no more than 28 radio stations nationally.
With the passage of the law and the relaxation of restrictions,
the radio industry has been in a state of upheaval as hundreds
of stations have been sold. Three firms in the largest radio
market now control access to more than half of the listening
audience. One of the firms, Clear Channel Communications,
owns 1,225 stations in the United States "and reaches . . .
more than 70 percent of the American public."[90]

Under proto-fascism, the marketplace of ideas has almost nothing to do with what is crucial for citizens to know in order to be active participants in shaping and sustaining a vibrant democracy. On the contrary, the media largely serve to target audiences for advertising, to pander to the anti-liberal ideologies of the political elite, to reinforce the conventional wisdom of corporate interests, and to promote cynical withdrawal by a populace adrift in a sea of celebrity scandal and mindless info-tainment. In a proto-fascist state, they deteriorate into a combination of commercialism, propaganda, and entertainment.[91] Under such circumstances, the media neither operate in the interests of the public good nor provide the pedagogical conditions necessary for producing critical citizens or defending a vibrant democracy. Instead, as McChesney and Nichols point out, concentrated media depoliticize the culture of politics, commercially carpet bomb its citizens, and denigrate public life.[92] Rather than perform an essential public service, they have become the primary tool for promoting a culture of consent in which citizens are misinformed and public discourse is debased. Media concentration restricts the range of views to which people have access and, in doing so, does a disservice to democracy itself. For example, "NOW with Bill Moyers" did a radio survey in which they discovered that "the top-rated talk radio stations across the country ran 310 hours of conservative talk each day and only five hours of views that were not rightwing."[93]

A fifth element of proto-fascism is the rise of an Orwellian version of Newspeak in the United States, or what Umberto Eco labels the language of "eternal fascism," whose purpose is to produce "an impoverished vocabulary, and an elementary syntax [whose consequence is] to limit the instruments for complex and critical reasoning."[94] Under the Bush Administration, especially since the horrible events of 9/11, the tools of language, sound, and image are increasingly being appropriated in an effort to diminish the capacity of the American public to think critically. As the critical power of language is reduced in official discourse to the simulacra of communication, it becomes more difficult for the American public to engage in critical debates, translate private considerations into public concerns, and recognize the distortions and lies that underlie much of the current government policies. What happens to critical language under the emergence of official Newspeak can be seen in the various ways in which the Bush Administration and its official supporters both misrepresent by misnaming government policies and simply engage in lying to cover up their own regressive politics and policies.[95]

Many people have pointed to Bush himself as a mangler of the English language, but this charge simply repeats the obvious while privatizing a much more important issue connecting language to power. Bush's discursive ineptness may be fodder for late-night comics, but such analyses miss the more strategic issue of how the Bush Administration actually manipulates discourse. For instance, Bush describes himself as a "reformer" while he promotes policies that expand corporate welfare, give tax benefits to the rich, and "erode the financial capacity of the state to undertake any but the most minimal welfare functions."[96] He defines himself as a "compassionate conservative," but he implements policies that result in "billions of dollars in cuts . . . proposed for food stamp and child nutrition programs, and for health care for the poor."[97] Bush's public speeches, often mimicked in the media, are filled with what Renana Brooks has called "empty language," that is, statements that are so abstract as to be relatively meaningless, except to reinforce in simplistic terms an often reactionary ideological position. Brooks cites the example of Bush's comment on the complex relationship between malpractice suits and skyrocketing health care, which he reduces to "No one has ever been healed by a frivolous lawsuit."[98] While Bush's own ideological position becomes clear in this comment, the complexity of the issue is completely trivialized and removed from public discussion.

Sometimes the distortions of official language are hard to miss, even among the media guards so quick to invoke patriotic correctness. One glaring example happened in an interview between Terry Gross, host of National Public Radio's "Fresh Air," and Grover Norquist, president of Americans for Tax Reform, also considered to be the chief architect of President Bush's tax plan. The topic for discussion was the estate tax, reviled as the "death tax" by conservative elites to gain popular support for its repeal, though the vast majority of Americans will not be affected by this tax. Gross suggested that because the estate tax affects only a small minority of people who get more than $2 million in inheritance, the law eliminating it clearly privileges the rich, not the average American. Norquist responded by arguing that the morality behind her argument was comparable to the same type of morality that resulted in the deaths of millions of Jews under the Holocaust. When Gross challenged this specious analogy, Norquist argued illogically that people (read liberals) who attacked the estate tax could now be placed on the same moral plane as the Nazis who killed more than six million Jews and untold others.[99] Under this logic, any critique of a minority group, but especially the rich, can be dismissed as being comparable to the kind of discrimination waged by the perpetrators of one of the worst mass murders in human history. Of course, there is the further implication that liberal critics should be punished for these views just as the Nazis were punished in Nuremberg for their crimes against humanity. This is not just a matter of using a desperate logic to dismiss counter-arguments, or of silencing one's critics through distortion, but actually demonizing those who hold the "wrong" views. Norquist's position is a contortion that fails to hide the fundamentalism that often drives this type of language.

Official Newspeak also trades in the rhetoric of fear in order to manipulate the public into a state of servile political dependency and unquestioning ideological support. Fear and its attendant use of moral panic create not only a rhetorical umbrella to promote other agendas, but also a sense of helplessness and cynicism throughout the body politic. Hence

Bush is increasingly dependent on issuing terror and security alerts, and panic-inducing references to 9/11 almost always are framed in Manichean language of absolute good and evil. Bush's doublespeak also employs the discourse of evangelicalism, with its attendant suggestion that whatever wisdom Bush has results from his direct communion with God — a position not unlike that of Moses on Mount Sinai — which, of course, cannot be challenged by mere mortals.[100]

While all governments sometimes resort to misrepresentations and lies, Bush's doublespeak makes such action central to its maintenance of political power and its manipulation of the media and the public. Language is used in this context to say one thing, but actually to mean its opposite.[101] This type of discourse mimics George Orwell's dystopian world of *1984*, in which the Ministry of Truth produces lies and the Ministry of Love tortures people. Ruth Rosen points out that the Bush Administration engages in a kind of doublespeak right out of Orwell's novel. For instance, Bush's Healthy Forest Initiative "allows increased logging of protected wilderness. The 'Clear Skies' initiative permits greater industrial air pollution."[102] With respect to the latter, the Bush Administration has produced Spanish-language public-service commercials hawking "Clear Skies" legislation, using ads that claim such legislation promotes "cleaner air," when in fact it has weakened restrictions on corporate polluters and eased regulations on some toxic emissions, such as mercury. In fact, J.P. Suarez, the Environmental Protection Agency's chief of enforcement, recently notified his staff that "the agency would stop pursuing Clean Air Act enforcement cases against coal burning power plants."[103] Eric Pianin reported in the *Washington Post* that "The Bush Administration has decided to allow thousands of the nation's dirtiest coal-fired power plants and refineries to upgrade their facilities without installing costly anti-pollution equipment as they now must do."[104] In addition, the Bush Administration has weakened federal programs for cleaning up dirty waters and has removed scientific studies offering evidence of global warming from government reports.[105]

Even when it comes to children, Bush is undaunted in his use of deceptive language. In arguing for legislation that would shift financial responsibility to the states for the highly successful Head Start program, which provides more than one million poor children with early education, health, and nutrition services, Bush employed the phrase "opt in" to encourage Congress to pass new legislation reforming Head Start. While "opt in" sounds as if it refers to expanding the program, it actually undermines it because the states that are facing crushing deficits do not have the money to fund the program. Thus the legislation would drastically weaken Head Start. Such language calls to mind the Orwellian logic that "war is peace, freedom is slavery, and ignorance is strength."

There is abundant evidence that the Bush Administration manipulated intelligence to legitimate its claim for a pre-emptive war with Iraq. The list of misrepresentations and rhetorical contortions includes the claims that Iraq was building nuclear weapons and producing biological and chemical agents and that Saddam Hussein was working with Osama bin Laden and had direct ties to Al Qaeda.[106] Even after the CIA reported that the charge that Saddam Hussein had bought uranium from the African country of Niger in pursuit of developing a nuclear weapon was fabricated, Bush included the assertion in his 2003 State of the Union Address.[107]

Charges of Newspeak do not come exclusively from the left or from cantankerous critics. *New York Times* op-ed writer and economist, Paul Krugman, asserts that "misrepresentation and deception are standard operating procedure for [the Bush] administration, which — to an extent never before seen in U.S. history — systematically and brazenly distorts the facts." Referring to Bush's record on the selling of the Iraqi war, he argues that it "is arguably the worst scandal in American political history — worse than Watergate, worse than Iran-contra. Indeed, the idea that we were deceived into war makes many commentators so uncomfortable that they refuse to admit the possibility."[108]

In what has to rank as either one of the most egregious distortions (or maybe just delusional ravings, as the *New York
Daily News* suggests)[109] that has emerged from the Bush Administration, President Bush, in an interview with *New Yorke*r
reporter Ken Auletta, claimed that "No president has ever
done more for human rights than I have."[110] Such a statement
is extraordinary given that Amnesty International condemned
the United States in 2002 for being one of the world leaders
in human rights violations. Similarly, a number of organizations, such as Human Rights Watch, U.S. Human Rights
Network, the ACLU, the Center for Constitutional Rights,
and Amnesty International, have accused the Bush Administration itself of engaging in various human rights violations,
including preventing foreign nationals held as prisoners at
Guantanamo Bay from gaining access to U.S. courts; execut-
ing juvenile offenders; engaging in the racial profiling, detention,
inhumane treatment, and deportation of Muslim immigrants
after 11 September 2001; and refusing to ratify the American
Convention on Human Rights, the Geneva Conventions, the
International Covenant on Civil and Political Rights, the
Convention on the Rights of the Child, and numerous other
international agreements aimed at protecting human rights.

A sixth element of proto-fascism is the growing collapse of
the separation between the church and state on the one hand,
and the increasing use of religious rhetoric as a marker of
political identity and the shaping of public policy on the
other. Religion has always played a powerful role in the daily
lives of Americans. But it never has wielded such influence in
the highest levels of American government as it does under
the Bush presidency. Moreover, the religious conservative
movement that has come into political prominence with the
election of George W. Bush views him as its earthly leader. As
*Washington Post* staff writer Dana Milbank, puts it:

> For the first time since religious conservatism became
> a modern political movement, the president of the

United States has become the movement's de facto leader
— a status even Ronald Reagan, though admired by religious conservatives, never earned. Christian publications,
radio and television shower Bush with praise, while
preachers from the pulpit treat his leadership as an act of
providence. A procession of religious leaders who have
met with him testify to his faith, while Web sites encourage people to fast and pray for the president.[111]

Considered the leader of the Christian right, Bush is viewed
by many of his aides and followers as a leader with a higher
purpose. Bush aide Tim Goeglein echoes this view: "I think
President Bush is God's man at this hour, and I say this with a
great sense of humility."[112] Ralph Reed, a long-time crusader
against divorce, single-parent families, and abortion and current head of Georgia's Republican Party, assesses Bush's relationship with the Christian right in more sobering political
terms. He argues that the role of the religious conservative
movement has changed in that it is no longer on the outskirts
of power since it has helped to elect leaders who believe in its
cause. Referring to the new-found role of the religious right,
he claims, "You're no longer throwing rocks at the building;
you're in the building."[113] Bush has not disappointed his radical evangelical Christian following.

President Bush openly celebrates the virtues of evangelical
Christian morality, prays daily, and expresses his fervent belief
in Christianity in both his rhetoric and policy choices. For
example, while running as a presidential candidate in 2000, Bush
proclaimed that his favorite philosopher was Jesus Christ.
Further, in a speech in which he outlined the dangers posed
by Iraq, he stated, "We do not claim to know all the ways of
Providence, yet we can trust in them, placing our confidence
in the loving God behind all of life, and all of history. May He
guide us now."[114] Stephen Mansfield, in *The Faith of George W.
Bush*, claims that Bush told James Robinson, a Texas preach-
er: "I feel like God wants me to run for president. I can't
explain it, but I sense my country is going to need me . . . . I

know it won't be easy on me or my family, but God wants me to do it."[115]

Bush relentlessly has developed policies based less on social needs than on a highly personal and narrow moral sense of divine purpose. Using the privilege of executive action, he has aggressively attempted to evangelize social services. For example, to a greater extent than any other president, he has made federal funds available to Christian religious groups that provide a range of social services. He also eased the rules "for overtly religious institutions to access $20-billion in federal social service grants and another $8-billion in Housing and Urban Development money. Tax dollars can now be used to construct and renovate houses of worship as long as the funds are not used to build the principal room used for prayer, such as the sanctuary or chapel."[116] He also provided more than $60 billion in federal funds for faith-based initiatives organized by religious charitable groups.[117]

However, not all religious groups receive equal funding. The lion's share of federal monies goes to Christian organizations, thus sanctioning some religions over others. In addition, he has promised that such agencies can get government funds "without being forced to change their character or compromise their mission."[118] This means that such organizations and groups can now get federal money even though they discriminate on religious grounds in their hiring practices. The two programs that Bush showcased during his January 2003 State of the Union speech both "use religious conversion as treatment."[119] Bush also has created an office in the White House dedicated entirely to providing assistance to faith-based organizations applying for federal funding.

Moreover, Bush is using school voucher programs to enable private schools to receive public money and is refusing to fund schools that "interfere with or fail to accommodate 'prayer or Bible study' by teachers or students."[120] The Secretary of Education, Rod Paige, made it clear how he feels about the separation of church and state when he told a Baptist publication that he believed that schools should teach Christian values. When asked to resign by a number of critics, Paige refused; and his office declined to clarify, if not repudiate, his suggestion that either public schools should teach Christian values or parents should take their kids out of such schools and send them to parochial schools. His office replied curtly: "The quotes are the quotes."[121]

The Bush Administration also refused to sign a United Nations declaration on children's rights, unless it eliminates such sexual health services as providing teenage sex education in which contraception or reproductive rights are discussed. On the domestic front, Bush has passed legislation halting "late-term" abortion, tried to pass legislation stopping the distribution of the morning-after pill, and eliminated financial support for international charities that provide advice on abortion. Such measures not only call into question the traditional separation between church and state, they also undercut public services and provide a veneer of government legitimacy to religious-based organizations that prioritize religious conversion over modern scientific techniques. As Winnifred Sullivan, a senior lecturer at the University of Chicago Divinity School, puts it, the conservative evangelical proponents of the faith-based initiative "want government funds to go to the kinds of churches that regard conversion as part of your rehabilitation. It's a critique of secular professional social service standards."[122]

Unfortunately, Bush's religious fervor appears more indebted to the God of the Old Testament, the God who believes in an eye for an eye, the God of vengeance and retribution. Hence Bush appears indifferent to the seeming contradiction between his claim to religious piety and his willingness as the governor of Texas to execute "more prisoners (152) than any governor in modern U.S. history."[123] Nor does he see the contradiction between upholding the word of God and imposing democracy on the largely Muslim population of Iraq through the rule of force and the barrel of a gun. Indeed, while Bush and his religious cohorts claim they are working to exercise great acts of charity, it appears that the poor are being punished and the only charity available is the handout given to the rich. For instance, as funds were being distributed for faith-based initiatives, Congress not only passed legislation that eliminated a child tax credit that would have benefitted about 2 million children, it also agreed to a $350 billion tax cut for the rich while slashing domestic spending for programs that benefit the poor, elderly, and children.

Bush is not the only one in his administration who combines evangelical morality with dubious ethical actions and undemocratic practices. Attorney General John Ashcroft, a Christian fundamentalist who holds morning-prayer sessions in his Washington office, added another layer to this type of religious fervor in February 2002 when he told a crowd at the National Religious Broadcasters Convention in Nashville, Tennessee, that the freedoms Americans enjoy appear to have little to do with the men who wrote the U.S. Constitution because such freedoms are made in Heaven. Ashcroft argues, "We are a nation called to defend freedom — a freedom that is not the grant of any government or document but is our endowment from God."[124] Without any irony intended, Ashcroft further exhibited his rigid Christian morality by having the "Spirit of Justice" statue draped in order to cover her marble breasts while, at the same time, violating the constitutional rights of thousands of Muslims and Arabs who, since 11 September 2001, he has arrested, held in secret, and offered no legal recourse or access to their families. Such harsh treatment rooted in a Manichean notion of absolute good and evil represents more than an act of capricious justice. It also undermines "the presumption of innocence, as well as the constitutional rights to due process, to counsel, and to a speedy and public trial"; and in legitimating such treatment, "the Bush administration has weakened these protections for all, citizens and aliens alike. In the process, it has tarnished American democracy."[125]

Behind the rhetoric of religious commitment is the reality of permanent war, the further immiseration of the poor, and ongoing attacks on the notion of the secular state. There is also the force of intolerance and bigotry, the refusal to recognize the multiplicity of religious, political, linguistic, and cultural differences — those vast and diverse elements that constitute the democratic global sphere at its best. Hints of this bigotry are visible not only in the culture of fear and religious fundamentalism that shapes the world of Bush and Ashcroft, but also in those who serve them with unquestioning loyalty. This became clear when the national press revealed that a high-ranking Defense Department official called the war on terrorism a Christian battle against Satan. Lt. General William Boykin, in his capacity as Deputy Under Secretary of Defense for Intelligence, while standing in front of pictures of Osama bin Laden, Saddam Hussein, and Kim Jung Il, asked the parishioners of the First Baptist church of Broken Arrow, Oklahoma, the following question: "Why do they hate us? . . . The answer to that is because we are a Christian nation. We are hated because we are a nation of believers." He continued, "Our spiritual enemy will only be defeated if we come against them in the name of Jesus."[126] For Boykin, it is a holy war being fought in Iraq, in Afghanistan, and, maybe, eventually at home against other nonbelievers. Boykin appears dead serious when claiming that other countries "have lost their morals, lost their values. But America is still a Christian nation."[127] This language is not merely the ranting of a religious fanatic; it is symptomatic of a deeper strain of intolerance and authoritarianism that is emerging in this country. It can be heard in the words of Reverend Jerry Falwell, who claimed on the airwaves that the terrorist attack of 9/11 was the result of God's judgment on the secularizing of America. Falwell stated: "I really believe that the pagans, and the abortionists, and the feminists, and the gays and lesbians, the ACLU, People for the American Way — all of them who have tried to secularize America — I point the finger in their face and say, 'You helped this happen'."[128]

The emergence of a government-sanctioned religious fundamentalism has its counterpart in a political authoritarianism that not only undermines the most basic tenets of religious faith but also the democratic tenets of social justice and equality. Of course, this type of religious fundamentalism, supported largely by politicians and evangelical missionaries who run the prayer groups and Bible study cells sprouting up all over the Bush White House, has little to do with genuine religion or spirituality. Those who believe that biblical creationism, rather than evolution, should be taught in the schools, or that the United States "must extend God's will of liberty for other countries, by force if necessary"[129] do not represent the prophetic traditions in Islam, Christianity, or Judaism. These traditions foster belief in a God who is giving and compassionate, who rejects secular policies that bankrupt the government in order to benefit the rich or that produce laws that disadvantage the poor and impose more suffering on those already in need. It is a tradition espoused by the Reverend James Forbes Jr., head of the Riverside Church in New York City, and captured in his assertion that "poverty is a weapon of mass destruction."[130] Joseph Hough, the head of Union Theological Seminary, speaks for many religious leaders when he argues that what passes as Christianity in the Bush Administration is simply a form of political machination masquerading as religion, making a grab for power. He writes:

> I'm getting tired of people claiming they're carrying the banner of my religious tradition when they're doing everything possible to undercut it. And that's what's happening in this country right now. The policies of this country are disadvantaging poor people every day of our lives and every single thing that passes the Congress these days is disadvantaging poor people more. . . . And anybody who claims in the name of God they're gonna run over people of other nations, and just willy-nilly, by your own free will, reshape the world in your own image, and claim that you're acting on behalf of God, that sounds a lot like Caesar to me.[131]

Apocalyptic biblical prophesies fuel more than the likes of John Ashcroft, who opposes dancing on moral grounds, or David Hager, appointed by Bush to the FDA's Advisory Committee for Reproductive Health Drugs, "who refuses to prescribe contraceptives to unmarried women (and believes the Bible is an antidote for premenstrual syndrome),"[132] they also fuel a worldview in which immigrants, African Americans, and others marked by differences in class, race, gender, and nationality are demonized, scapegoated, and subjected to acts of state violence. Such rhetoric and the policies it supports need to be recognized as a crisis of democracy itself. What progressives and others need to acknowledge is that the Bush Administration's attempt to undo the separation between church and state is driven by a form of fundamentalism that both discredits democratic values, public goods, and critical citizenship and spawns an irrationality evident in the innumerable contradictions between its rhetoric of "compassionate conservative" religious commitment and its relentless grab for economic and political power — an irrationality that is the hallmark of both the old fascism and proto-fascism.

While there are other elements central to proto-fascism, I want to conclude in substantial detail with a discussion of the growing militarization of public space and the social order in American society. Of course, the militarization of public space was a central feature of the old fascism. This feature is particularly important in the United States because it poses the greatest risk to our civil liberties and any semblance of democracy, and because it has been a crucial force in the rise of the national security state.

# The Politics
# of Militarization
# at Home and Abroad

Militarization refers to increasing centrality of the military in American society, the militarization of U.S. culture, and the increased propensity to suppress dissent. The process of militarization has a long history in the United States and is varied, rather than static, and changes under different historical conditions.[133] My use of the term comes from Michael S. Sherry, who defines it as "the process by which war and national security became consuming anxieties and provided memories, models, and metaphors that shaped broad areas of national life."[134] Unlike the old style of militarization in which all forms of civil authority are subordinate to military authority, the new ethos of militarization is organized to engulf the entire social order, legitimating its values as a central aspect of American public life. Moreover, the values of militarism no longer reside in a single group or are limited to a particular sphere of society. On the contrary, as Jorge Mariscal points out:

> In liberal democracies, in particular, the values of militarism do not reside in a single group but are diffused across a wide variety of cultural locations. In twenty-first

century America, no one is exempt from militaristic values
because the processes of militarization allow those values
to permeate the fabric of everyday life.[135]

Popular fears about domestic safety and internal threats
accentuated by endless terror alerts have created a society that
increasingly accepts the notion of a "war without limits" as a
normal state of affairs. But fear and insecurity do more than
produce a collective anxiety among Americans. Fear is used to
maufacture political loyalty, exploited largely to get citizens to
believe that they should vote Republican because it is the only
political party that can protect Americans. Such fears also can
be manipulated into a kind of "war fever." The mobilization
of war fever, intensified through a politics of fear, carries with
it a kind of paranoid edge, endlessly stoked by government
alerts and repressive laws and used "to create the most extensive national security apparatus in our nation's history."[136] This
war fever is also reproduced in the media, which also have
helped to create a civil society that has become more aggressive in its warlike enthusiasms. But there is more at work here
than simply exploiting war for higher ratings or the attempts
by right-wing political strategists to keep the American public
in a state of permanent fear in order to remove pressing
domestic issues from public debate. There is also the attempt
by the Bush Administration to convince as many Americans as
possible that under the current "state of emergency," the use
of the military internally in domestic affairs is perfectly
acceptable, evident in the increasing propensity to use the
military establishment "to incarcerate and interrogate suspected terrorists and 'enemy combatants' and keep them
beyond the reach of the civilian judicial system, even if they
are American citizens."[137] This is evident in the federal government's attempts to try terrorists in military courts and to
detain prisoners "outside the provisions of the Geneva
Convention as prisoners of war . . . at the U.S. Marine Corps
base at Guantanamo, Cuba because that facility is outside of
the reach of the American courts."[138]

Militarization abroad cannot be separated from the inc ing militarization of society at home. War takes on a . meaning in American life as wars are waged on drugs, soual policies are criminalized, youth are tried as adults, incarceration rates soar among the poor and people of color, and schools are increasingly modeled after prisons.

The rampant combination of fear and insecurity that is so much a part of the permanent war culture in the United States seems to bear down particularly hard on children. In many poor school districts, specialists are being laid off and crucial mental health services are being cut back. As Sara Rimer recently pointed out in the *New York Times*, much needed student-based services and traditional, if not compassionate, ways of dealing with student problems are being replaced by the juvenile justice system, which functions "as a dumping ground for poor minority kids with mental health and special-education problems. . . . The juvenile detention center has become an extension of the principal's office."[139] For example, in some cities, ordinances have been passed that "allow for the filing of misdemeanor charges against students for anything from disrupting a class to assaulting a teacher."[140] Children no longer are given a second chance for minor behavior infractions, nor are they simply sent to the guidance counselor, the principal, or to detention. They now come under the jurisdiction of the courts and juvenile justice system.

The militarization of public high schools has become so commonplace that even in the face of the most flagrant disregard for children's rights, such acts are justified by both administrators and the public on the grounds that they keep kids safe. In Biloxi, Mississippi, surveillance cameras have been installed in all of its 500 classrooms. The school's administrators call this "school reform," but none of them have examined the implications of what they are teaching kids who are put under constant surveillance. The not-so-hidden curriculum is that kids can't be trusted and that their rights are not worth protecting. At the same time, they are being educated to passively accept military-sanctioned practices organized around main-taining control, surveillance, and unquestioned authority, all conditions central to a police state and proto-fascism.

It gets worse. Some schools are using sting operations in which undercover agents pretend to be students in order to catch young people suspected of selling drugs or committing any of a number of school infractions. The consequences of such actions are far reaching. As Randall Beger points out:

> Opponents of school-based sting operations say they not only create a climate of mistrust between students and police, but they also put innocent students at risk of wrongful arrest due to faulty tips and overzealous police work. When asked about his role in a recent undercover probe at a high school near Atlanta, a young-looking police officer who attended classes and went to parties with students replied: "I knew I had to fit in, make kids trust me and then turn around and take them to jail."[141]

Instances of domestic militarization and the war at home also can be seen in the rise of the prison-industrial-educational complex and the militarization of the criminal justice system. The traditional "distinctions between military, police, and criminal justice are blurring."[142] The police now work in close collaboration with the military. This takes the form of re-ceiving surplus weapons, arranging technology/information transfers, introducing SWAT teams modeled after the Navy Seals — which are experiencing a steep growth in police departments throughout the United States — and becoming more dependent on military models of crime control.[143] The increasing use of such military models in American life has played a crucial role in the paramilitarizing of the culture, which provides both a narrative and legitimation "for recent trends in corrections, including the normalization of special response teams, the increasingly popular Supermax prisons, and drug war boot camps."[144] In the paramilitaristic perspec-tive, crime is no longer seen as a social problem. Crime now is viewed as both an individual pathology and a matter of punishment, rather than rehabilitation.

Unsurprisingly, paramilitary culture increasingly embodies a racist and class-specific discourse and "reflects the discrediting of the social and its related narratives."[145] This is particularly evident as America's inner cities are being singled out as dangerous enclaves of crime and violence. The consequences for those communities have been catastrophic, especially in terms of the cataclysmic rise of the prison-industrial complex. As is widely reported, the United States is now the biggest jailer in the world. Between 1985 and 2002 the prison population grew from 744,206 to 2.1 million (approaching the combined populations of Idaho, Wyoming, and Montana), and prison budgets jumped from $7 billion in 1980 to $40 billion in 2000.[146] As Sanho Tree, points out:

> With more than 2 million people behind bars (there are only 8 million prisoners in the entire world), the United States — with one-twenty-second of the world's population — has one-quarter of the planet's prisoners. We operate the largest penal system in the world, and approximately one-quarter of all our prisoners (nearly half a million people) are there for nonviolent drug offenses.[147]

Yet, even as the crime rate plummets dramatically, more people, especially those of color, are being arrested, harassed, punished, and put in jail.[148] Of the two million people behind bars, 70% of the inmates are people of color: 50% are African American and 17% are Latino.[149] A Justice Department report points out and that on any give day in this country, "more than a third of the young African-American men aged 18-34 in some of our major cities are either in prison or under some form of criminal justice supervision."[150] The same department reported in April 2000 that "black youth are forty-eight times more likely than whites to be sentenced to juvenile prison for drug offenses."[151] When poor youth of color are not being warehoused in dilapidated schools or incarcerated, they are being aggressively recruited by the Army to fight the war in Iraq. For example, Carl Chery recently reported:

> With help from *The Source* magazine, the U.S. military is targeting hip-hop fans with custom made Hummers, throwback jerseys and trucker hats. The yellow Hummer, spray-painted with two black men in military uniform, is the vehicle of choice for the U.S. Army's "Take It to the Streets campaign" — a sponsored mission aimed at recruiting young African Americans into the military ranks.[152]

It seems that the Army has discovered hip-hop and urban culture and, rather than listening to the searing indictments of poverty, joblessness, and despair that is one of its central messages, the Army recruiters appeal to its most commodified elements by letting the "potential recruits hang out in the Hummer, where they can pep the sound system or watch recruitment videos"[153] Of course, they won't view any videos of Hummers being blown up in the war-torn streets of Baghdad.

Under the auspices of the national security state and owing to the militarization of domestic life, containment policies become the principle means to discipline working-class youth and restrict their ability to think critically and engage in oppositional practices. Marginalized students learn quickly that they are surplus populations and that the journey from home to school no longer means they will next move into a job; on the contrary, school now becomes a training ground for their "graduation" into such containment centers as prisons and jails that keep them out of sight, patrolled, and monitored in order to prevent them from becoming a social canker or political liability to those white and middle-class populations concerned about their own safety. Schools increasingly function as zoning mechanisms to separate students marginalized by class and color; and, as such, these institutions now are modeled after prisons. This follows the argument of David Garland, who points out, "Large-scale incarceration functions as a mode of economic and social placement, a zoning mechanism that segregates those populations rejected by the depleted institutions of family, work, and welfare and places them behind the scenes of social life."[154]

Judging from Bush's 2004 State of the Union Address, the Bush Administration will continue to allocate funds for "educational reform" intended both to strip young people of the capacity to think critically by teaching them that learning is largely about taking tests and to prepare them for a culture in which punishment has become the central principle of reform. Bush cannot fully fund his own education reform act, but he pledged in his 2004 State of the Union Address an additional 23 million dollars to promote drug testing of students in public schools. In short, fear, punishment, and containment continue to override the need to provide health care for 9.3 million uninsured children, increase the ranks of new teachers by at least 100,000, fully support Head Start programs, repair deteriorating schools, and improve those youth services that, for many poor students, would provide an alternative to the direct pipeline between school and the local police station, the courts, or prison.

Domestic militarization, also widespread in the realm of culture, functions as a mode of public pedagogy, instilling the values and the aesthetic of militarization through a wide variety of pedagogical sites and cultural venues. For instance, Humvee ads offer up the fantasy of military glamour and modes of masculinity, marketed to suggest that ownership of these vehicles, first used in Desert Storm, not only guarantees virility for their owners but also promotes a mixture of fear and admiration from everyone else. One of the fastest-growing sports for middle-class suburban youth is the game of paintball "in which teenagers stalk and shoot each other on 'battlefields' (In San Diego, paintball participants pay an additional $50 to hone their skills at the Camp Pendleton Marine Base)."[155] And military recruitment ads flood all modes of entertainment and use sophisticated marketing tools that offer messages with a strong appeal to the hyper-masculinity of young men. Such ads resonate powerfully with the appeal to particular forms of masculinity that directly serve as an enticement for recruitment. For example, the website, www.marines.com, opens with the sound of gunfire and then provides the following message:

> We are the warriors, one and all. Born to defend, built to conquer. The steel we wear is the steel within ourselves, forged by the hot fires of discipline and training. We are fierce in a way no other can be. We are the marines.

From video games to Hollywood films to children's toys, popular culture increasingly is bombarded with militarized values, symbols, and images. Such video games as *Doom* have a long history of using violent graphics and shooting techniques that appeal to the most extreme modes of masculinity. The Marine Corps was so taken with *Doom* in the mid-1990s that it produced its own version of the game, *Marine Doom*, and made it available to download for free. One of the developers of the game, Lieutenant Scott Barnett, claimed at the time that it was a useful game to keep marines entertained.

The interface of military and popular culture not only is valuable in providing videogame technology for diverse military uses, it also has resulted in the armed forces developing partnerships "with the video game industry to train and recruit soldiers."[156] The military uses the games to train recruits, and the videogame makers offer products that have the imprimatur of a first-class fighting machine. And the popularity of militarized war games is on the rise. Nick Turse argues that as the line between entertainment and war disappears, a "'military-entertainment complex' [has] sprung up to feed both the military's desire to bring out ever-more-realistic computer and video combat games. Through video games, the military and its partners in academia and the entertainment industry are creating an arm of media culture geared toward preparing young Americans for armed conflict."[157]

Combat teaching games offer a perfect fit between the Pentagon, with its accelerating military budget, and the entertainment industry, with annual revenues of $479 billion, including $40 billion from the videogame industry. The entertainment industry offers a stamp of approval for the Pentagon's war games, and the Defense Department provides an aura of authenticity for corporate America's war-based products. Collaboration between the Defense Department and the entertainment industry has been going on since 1997, but the permanent war culture that now grips the United States has given this partnership a new life and has greatly expanded its presence in popular culture.

The military has found numerous ways to take advantage of the intersection between popular culture and the new electronic technologies. Such technologies are being employed not only to train military personnel, but also to attract recruits, tapping into the realm of popular culture with its celebration of videogames, computer technology, the Internet, and other elements of visual culture used by teenagers.[158] For example, the army has developed online software that appeals to computer-literate recruits, and the most attractive feature of the software is a shooting game "that actually simulates battle and strategic-warfare situations."[159] When asked about the violence being portrayed, Brian Ball, the lead developer of the game, was clear about its purpose. "We don't downplay the fact that the Army manages violence. We hope that this will help people understand the role of the military in American life."[160]

Capitalizing on its link with industry, the military now has a host of new war games in production. For instance, there is *America's Army*, one of the most popular and successful recruiting videogames. This game teaches young people how "to kill enemy soldiers while wearing your pajamas [and also provides] plenty of suggestions about visiting your local recruiter and joining the real US Army."[161] Using the most updated versions of satellite technology, military-industry collaboration also has produced *Kuma: War*. This game was developed by the Department of Defense and Kuma Reality

⌐ames and slated for release in 2004. It is a subscription-based product that "prepares gamers for actual missions based on real-world conflicts," updated weekly.[162] The game allows players to recreate actual news stories, such as the raid American forces conducted in Mosul, Iraq, in which Saddam Hussein's two sons, Uday and Qusay, were killed. Gamers can take advantage of real "true to life satellite imagery and authentic military intelligence, to jump from the headlines right into the frontlines of international conflict."[163] Of course, the realities of carrying 80-pound knapsacks in 120-degree heat, the panic-inducing fear of real people shooting real bullets or planting real bombs to kill or maim you and your fellow soldiers, and the months or years away from family are not among those experiences reproduced for instruction or entertainment.

Young people no longer learn military values in training camps or in military-oriented schools. These values now are disseminated through the pedagogical force of popular culture itself, which has become a major tool used by the armed forces to educate young people about the ideology and social relations that inform military life — minus a few of the unpleasantries. The collaboration between the military and the entertainment industry offers up a form of public pedagogy that "may help to produce great battlefield decision makers, but . . . strike from debate the most crucial decisions young people can make in regard to the morality of a war — choosing whether or not to fight and for what cause."[164]

The popularity of militarized culture is apparent not only in the sales of video combat games, but also in the sales of children's toys. Major retailers and major chain stores across the country are selling out of war-related toys. In one day, the KB Toys stores in San Antonio, Texas, sold out an entire shipment of fatigue-clad plush hamsters that dance to military music; and managers at KB Toys stores were instructed "to feature military toys in the front of their stores."[165] Sales of action figures also have soared. "Between 2001 and 2002, sales of *G.I.*

*Joe* increased by 46 percent, as Hasbro reported. And when toy retailer Small Blue Planet launched a series of figures called 'Special forces: Showdown With Iraq,' two of the four models sold out immediately."[166] KB Toys took advantage of the infatuation with action toys related to the war in Iraq by marketing a doll that is a pint-sized model of George W. Bush dressed in the pilot regalia he wore when he landed on the USS Abraham Lincoln on 1 May 2003. Japanese electronic giant Sony attempted to cash in on the war in Iraq by trademarking the phrase "Shock and Awe" for use with video and computer games. The phrase was used by Pentagon strategists as part of a scare tactic to be used against Iraq. In addition, the *New York Times* reported that after 11 September 2001, "nearly two-dozen applications were filed for the phrase, 'Let's Roll.'" The term was made famous by one of the passengers on the ill-fated plane that was hijacked and crashed in a field in Pennsylvania.

Even in the world of fashion, the ever-spreading chic of militarization and patriotism is making its mark. Army-Navy stores are doing a brisk business selling not only American flags, gas masks, aviator sunglasses, night-vision goggles, and other military equipment, but also clothing with the camouflage look.[167] Even top designers are getting into the act. For example, at a recent fashion show in Milan, Italy, many designers were "drawn to G.I. uniforms [and were] fascinated by the construction of military uniforms." One designer "had beefy models in commando gear scramble over tabletops and explode balloons."[168]

Proto-fascism views life as a form of permanent warfare and, in doing so, subordinates society to the military, rather than viewing the military as subordinate to the needs of a democratic social order. Militarism in this scenario diminishes both the legitimate reasons for a military presence in society and the necessary struggle for the promise of democracy itself. As Umberto Eco points out, under the rubric of its aggressive militarism, proto-fascist ideology maintains that "there is no struggle for life but, rather, life is lived for struggle."[169]

The ideology of militarization is central to any understanding of proto-fascism because it appeals to a form of irrationality that is at odds with any viable notion of democracy. Militarization uses fear to drive human behavior, and the values it promotes are mainly distrust, patriarchy, and intolerance. Within this ideology, masculinity is associated with violence, and action often is substituted for the democratic processes of deliberation and debate. Militarization as an ideology is about the rule of force and the expansion of repressive state power. In fact, democracy appears as an excess in this logic and often is condemned by militarists as being a weak system of government.

Echoes of this anti-democratic sentiment can be found in the passage of the Patriot Act with its violation of civil liberties, in the rancorous patriotism that equates dissent with treason, and in the discourse of public commentators who, in the fervor of a militarized culture, fan the flames of hatred and intolerance. One example that has become all too typical emerged after the 9/11 attacks. Columnist Ann Coulter, in calling for a holy war on Muslims, wrote, "We should invade their countries, kill their leaders and convert them to Christianity. We weren't punctilious about locating and punishing only Hitler and his top officers. We carpet-bombed German cities; we killed civilians. That's war. And this is war."[170] While this statement does not reflect mainstream American opinion, the uncritical and chauvinistic patriotism and intolerance that informs it not only have become standard fare among many conservative radio hosts in the United States, but increasingly are being legitimated in a variety of cultural venues.

As militarization spreads through the culture, it produces policies that rely more on force than on dialogue and compassion. It offers up modes of identification that undermine democratic values and tarnish civil liberties, and it makes the production of both symbolic and material violence a central feature of everyday life. As Kevin Baker points out, we are quickly becoming a nation that "substitute[s] military solutions for almost everything, including international alliances, diplomacy, effective intelligence agencies, democratic institutions — even national security."[171] By blurring the lines between military and civilian functions, militarization deforms our language, debases democratic values, celebrates fascist modes of control, defines citizens as soldiers, and diminishes our ability as a nation to uphold international law and support a democratic global public sphere. Unless militarization is systematically exposed and resisted at every place where it appears in the culture, it will undermine the meaning of critical citizenship and do great harm to those institutions that are central to a democratic society.

# Neoliberalism and the Death of Democracy

> Neo-liberalism has changed the fundamental nature of politics. Politics used to be primarily about who ruled whom and who got what share of the pie. Aspects of both these central questions remain, of course; but the great new central question of politics is "Who has a right to live and who does not?" Radical exclusion is now the order of the day.[172]

It is almost impossible to understand the rise of such multi-faceted authoritarianism in American society without analyzing the importance of neoliberalism as the defining ideology of the current historical moment.[173] While fascism does not need neoliberalism to develop, neoliberalism creates the ideological and economic conditions that can promote a uniquely American version of fascism.[174] Neoliberalism not only undermines the vital economic and political institutions and public spaces central to a democracy, it also has no vocabulary for recognizing anti-democratic forms of power. Even worse, it accentuates a structural relationship between the state and the economy that produces hierarchies, concentrates power in relatively few hands, unleashes the most brutal elements of a rabid individualism, destroys the welfare state, incarcerates large numbers of its disposable population, economically disenfranchises large segments of the lower and middle classes, and reduces entire countries to pauperization.[175]

Under neoliberalism, the state now makes a grim alignment with corporate capital and transnational corporations. Gone are the days when the state "assumed responsibility for a range of social needs."[176] Instead, agencies of government now pursue a wide range of "'deregulations,' privatizations, and abdications of responsibility to the market and private philanthropy."[177] Deregulation promotes "widespread, systematic disinvestment in the nation's basic productive capacity."[178] Flexible production encourages wage slavery at home. And the search for ever-greater profits leads to outsourcing, which accentuates the flight of capital and jobs abroad. Neoliberalism has now become the prevailing logic in the United States; and according to Stanley Aronowitz, "the neoliberal economic doctrine proclaiming the superiority of free markets over public ownership, or even public regulation of private economic activities, has become the conventional wisdom, not only among conservatives but among social progressives."[179]

The ideology and power of neoliberalism also cut across national boundaries. Throughout the globe, the forces of neoliberalism are on the march, dismantling the historically guaranteed social provisions provided by the welfare state, defining profit-making as the essence of democracy, and equating freedom with the unrestricted ability of markets to "govern economic relations free of government regulation."[180] Transnational in scope, neoliberalism now imposes its economic regime and market values on developing and weaker nations through structural adjustment policies enforced by such powerful financial institutions as the World Bank, the International Monetary Fund (IMF), and the World Trade Organization (WTO). Secure in its dystopian vision that there are no alternatives, as Margaret Thatcher once put it, neoliberalism obviates issues of contingency, struggle, and social agency by celebrating the inevitability of economic laws in which the ethical ideal of intervening in the world gives way to the idea that we "have no choice but to adapt both our hopes and our abilities to the new global market."[181] Coupled with a new culture of fear, market freedoms seem securely grounded in a defense of national security, capital, and property rights.

In its capacity to dehistoricize and depoliticize society, as well as its aggressive attempts to destroy all of the public spheres necessary for the defense of a genuine democracy, neoliberalism reproduces the conditions for unleashing the most brutalizing forces of capitalism and accentuating the most central elements of proto-fascism. As the late Pierre Bourdieu argued, neoliberalism is a policy of depoliticization, attempting to liberate the economic sphere from all government controls.

> Drawing shamelessly on the lexicon of liberty, liberalism, and deregulation, it aims to grant economic determinisms a fatal stranglehold by liberating them from all controls, and to obtain the submission of citizens and governments to the economic and social forces thus liberated. . . . [T]his policy has imposed itself through the most varied means, especially juridical, on the liberal — or even social democratic — governments of a set of economically advanced countries, leading them gradually to divest themselves of the power to control economic forces.[182]

At the same time, neoliberalism uses the breathless rhetoric of the global victory of free-market rationality to cut public expenditures and undermine those non-commodified public spheres that serve as the repository for critical education, language, and public intervention. Spewed forth by the mass media, right-wing intellectuals, and governments alike, neoliberal ideology, with its ongoing emphasis on deregulation and privatization, has found its material expression in an all-out attack on democratic values and on the very notion of the public sphere. Within the discourse of neoliberalism, the notion of the public good is devalued and, where possible, eliminated as part of a wider rationale for a handful of private interests to control as much of social life as possible in order to maximize their personal profit. Public services, such as health care, child care, public assistance, education, and transportation, now are subject to the rules of the market. Construing the public good as a private good and the needs of the corporate and private sector as the only source of investment, neoliberal ideology produces, legitimates, and exacerbates the existence of persistent poverty, inadequate health care, racial apartheid in the inner cities, and the growing inequalities between the rich and the poor.[183]

As Stanley Aronowitz points out, the Bush Administration has made neoliberal ideology the cornerstone of its program and has been in the forefront in actively supporting and implementing the following policies:

> deregulation of business at all levels of enterprises and trade; tax reduction for wealthy individuals and corporations; the revival of the near-dormant nuclear energy industry; limitations and abrogation of labor's right to organize and bargain collectively; a land policy favoring commercial and industrial development at the expense of conservation and other proenvironment policies; elimination of income support to the chronically unemployed; reduced federal aid to education and health; privatization of the main federal pension programs, Social Security; limitation on the right of aggrieved individuals to sue employers and corporations who provide services; in addition, as social programs are reduced, [Republicans] are joined by the Democrats in favoring increases in the repressive functions of the state, expressed in the dubious drug wars in the name of fighting crime, more funds for surveillance of ordinary citizens, and the expansion of the federal and local police forces.[184]

Central to both neoliberal ideology and its implementation by the Bush Administration are the ongoing attempts by free-market fundamentalists and right-wing politicians to view government as the enemy of freedom (except when it aids big business) and to discount it as a guardian of the public interest. The call to eliminate big government is neoliberalism's great unifying idea and has broad popular appeal in the United States because it is a principle deeply embedded in the country's history and tangled up with its notion of political freedom. And yet the right-wing appropriation of this tradition is filled with contradictions in terms of neoliberal policies. As William Greider points out:

> "Leave me alone" is an appealing slogan, but the right regularly violates its own guiding principle. The anti-abortion folks intend to use government power to force their own moral values on the private lives of others. Free-market right-wingers fall silent when Bush and congress intrude to bail out airlines, insurance companies, banks — whatever sector finds itself in desperate need. The hard-right conservatives are downright enthusiastic when the Supreme Court and Bush's Justice Department hack away at our civil liberties. The "school choice" movement seeks not smaller government but a vast expansion of taxpayer obligations.[185]

The advocates of neoliberalism have attacked what they call big government when it has provided such essential services as crucial safety nets for the less fortunate, but they have no qualms about using the government to bail out the airline industry after the economic nosedive that followed the 2000 election of George W. Bush and the events of 9/11. Nor are there any expressions of outrage from the cheerleaders of neoliberalism when the state engages in promoting various forms of corporate welfare by providing billions of dollars in direct and indirect subsidies to multinational corporations. In short, government bears no obligation for either the poor and dispossessed or for the collective future of young people.

As the laws of the market take precedence over the laws of the state as guardians of the public good, the government increasingly offers little help in mediating the interface between the advance of capital and its rapacious commercial interests. Neither does it aid non-commodified interests and nonmarket spheres that create the political, economic, and social spaces and discursive conditions vital for critical citizenship and democratic public life. Within the discourse of neoliberalism, it becomes difficult for the average citizen to speak about political or social transformation or even to challenge, outside of a grudging nod toward rampant corruption, the ruthless downsizing, the ongoing liquidation of job security, or the elimination of benefits for people now hired on a part-time basis.

The liberal democratic vocabulary of rights, entitlements, social provisions, community, social responsibility, living wage, job security, equality, and justice seem oddly out of place in a country where the promise of democracy has been replaced by casino capitalism, a winner-take-all philosophy suited to lotto players and day traders alike. As corporate culture extends even deeper into the basic institutions of civil and political society, buttressed daily by a culture industry largely in the hands of concentrated capital, it is reinforced even further by the pervasive fear and insecurity of the public by the deep-seated skepticism in the public mind that the future holds nothing beyond a watered-down version of the present. As the prevailing discourse of neoliberalism seizes the public imagination, there is no vocabulary for progressive social change, democratically inspired visions, or critical notions of social agency to expand the meaning and purpose of democratic public life. Against the reality of low-wage jobs, the erosion of social provisions for a growing number of people, and the expanding war against young people of color at home and empire-building abroad, the market-driven juggernaut of neoliberalism continues to mobilize desires in the interest of producing market identities and market relationships that ultimately sever the link between education and social change while reducing agency to the obligations of consumerism.

As neoliberal ideology and corporate culture extend even deeper into the basic institutions of civil and political society, there is a simultaneous diminishing of non-commodified public spheres — such institutions as public schools, independent bookstores, churches, noncommercial public broadcasting stations, libraries, trade unions, and various voluntary institutions engaged in dialogue, education, and learning — that address the relationship of the individual to public life and foster social responsibility and provide a robust vehicle for public participation and democratic citizenship. As media theorists Edward Herman and Robert McChesney observe, noncommodified public spheres historically have played an invaluable role "as places and forums where issues of importance to a political community are discussed and debated, and where information is presented that is essential to citizen participation in community life."[186] Without these critical public spheres, corporate power often goes unchecked and politics becomes dull, cynical, and oppressive.[187] Moreover, in the vacuum left by diminishing democracy, it is religious zealotry, cultural chauvinism, xenophobia, and racism that have become the dominant tropes of neoconservatives and other extremist groups eager to take advantage of the growing insecurity, fear, and anxiety that result from increased joblessness, the war on terror, and the unraveling of communities. In this context, neoliberalism creates the economic, social, and political instability that helps feed both the neoconservative and religious right movements and their proto-fascist policy initiatives.

Especially troubling under the rule of neoliberalism is not simply that ideas associated with freedom and agency are defined through the prevailing ideology and principles of the market, but that neoliberal ideology also wraps itself in what appears to be an unassailable appeal to conventional wisdom. Defined as the paragon of modern social relations by Friedrich A. von Hayek, Milton Friedman, Robert Nozick, Francis Fukuyama, and other market fundamentalists, neoliberalism attempts to eliminate any engaged critique about its most basic principles and social consequences by embracing the "market as the arbiter of social destiny."[188] Neoliberalism empties the public treasury, privatizes formerly public services, limits the vocabulary and imagery available to recognize anti-democratic forms of power, and reinforces narrow models of individual agency. Equally important is its role in undermining the critical functions of a viable democracy by undercutting the ability of individuals to engage in the continuous translation between public considerations and private interests, which it accomplishes, in part, by collapsing public issues into the realm of the private. As Bauman observes, "It is no longer true that the 'public' is set on colonizing the 'private'. The opposite is the case: it is the private that colonizes the public space, squeezing out and chasing away everything which cannot be fully, without residue, translated into the vocabulary of private interests and pursuits."[189] Divested of its political possibilities and social underpinnings, freedom offers few opportunities for people to translate private worries into public concerns and collective struggle.[190]

The good life, in this discourse, "is construed in terms of our identities as consumers — we are what we buy."[191] For example, some neoliberal advocates argue that the healthcare and education crises faced by many states can be solved by selling off public assets to private interests. Blatantly demonstrating neoliberal ideology's contempt for non-commodified public spheres and democratic values, the Pentagon even considered, if only for a short time, turning the war on terror and security concerns over to futures markets, subject to online trading. In this exhibition of market logic and casino capitalism, neoliberalism reveals its dream of a social order dominated by commercial spheres. At the same time, it aggressively attempts to empty the substance of critical democracy and replace it with a democracy of goods available to those with purchasing power and the ability to expand the cultural and political power of corporations throughout the world. As a result of the consolidated corporate attack on public life, the maintenance of democratic public spheres from which to launch a moral vision or to engage in a viable struggle over politics loses all credibility — not to mention monetary support. As the alleged objectivity of neoliberal ideology remains largely unchallenged within dominant public spheres, individual critique and collective political struggles become more difficult.[192] It gets worse. Dominated by extremists, the Bush Administration is driven by an arrogance of power and inflated sense of moral righteousness mediated largely by a false sense of certitude and never-ending posture of triumphalism. As George Soros points out, this rigid ideology and inflexible sense of mission allows the Bush Administration to believe that "because we are stronger than others, we must know better and we must have right on our side. This is where religious fundamentalism comes together with market fundamentalism to form the ideology of American supremacy."[193]

As public space is increasingly commodified and the state becomes more closely aligned with capital, politics is defined largely by its policing functions, rather than as an agency for peace and social reform. Its ideological counterpart is a public pedagogy that mobilizes power in the interest of a social order marked by the progressive removal of autonomous spheres of cultural production, such as journalism, publishing, and film; by the destruction of collective structures capable of counteracting the widespread imposition of commercial values and the effects of the pure market; by the creation of a global reserve army of the unemployed; and by the subordination of nation-states to the real masters of the economy. Bourdieu emphasizes the effects of neoliberalism on this dystopian world:

> First is the destruction of all the collective institutions capable of counteracting the effects of the infernal machine, primarily those of the state, repository of all of the universal values associated with the idea of the public realm. Second is the imposition everywhere, in the upper spheres of the economy and the state as at the heart of corporations, of that sort of moral Darwinism that, with the cult of the winner, schooled in higher mathematics and bungee jumping, institutes the struggle of all against all and cynicism as the norm of all action and behaviour.[194]

Besides the destruction of collective solidarities, though never without opposition, neoliberalism refigures the relationship between the state and capital. As the state abandons its social investments in health, education, and the public welfare, it becomes progressively reduced to its repressive functions. Such theorists as George Steinmetz, Pierre Bourdieu, Howard Zinn, Stanley Aronowitz, and Noam Chomsky have argued that as the state is hollowed out, it increasingly takes on the functions of an enhanced police state or security state, the signs of which are most visible in the increasing use of the state apparatus to spy on and arrest its subjects, the incarceration of individuals considered disposable (primarily poor people of color), and the ongoing criminalization of social policies. Examples of the last include anti-begging and anti-loitering ordinances that fine or punish homeless people for sitting or lying down too long in public places.[195] An even more despicable instance of the barbaric nature of neoliberalism — with its emphasis on profits over people and its willingness to punish, rather than serve, the poor and disenfranchised — can be seen in the growing tendency of many hospitals across the country to have patients arrested and jailed if they cannot pay their medical bills. This policy, right out of the pages of George Orwell's *1984*, represents a return to debtors prisons. Now chillingly called "body attachment," it is "basically a warrant for . . . the patient's arrest."[196]

Neoliberalism is not simply an economic policy designed to cut government spending, pursue free-trade policies, and free market forces from government regulations; it is also a political philosophy and ideology that affects every dimension of social life. Neoliberalism has heralded a radical economic, political, and experiential shift that now largely defines the citizen as a consumer, disbands the social contract in the interests of privatized considerations, and separates capital from the context of place. Within this discourse, as Jean and John Comaroff have argued, "the personal is the only politics there is, the only politics with a tangible referent or emotional valence. It is in these privatized terms that action is organized, that the experience of inequity and antagonism takes meaningful shape."[197] Under such circumstances, neoliberalism portends the death of politics as we know it, strips the social of its democratic values, reconstructs agency in terms that are utterly privatized, and provides the conditions for an emerging form of proto-fascism that must be resisted at all costs. Neoliberalism not only enshrines unbridled individualism as a central feature of proto-fascism, as Herbert Marcuse reminds us,[198] it also destroys any vestige of democratic society by undercutting its "moral, material, and regulatory moorings."[199] In doing so, it offers no language for understanding how the future might be grasped outside of the narrow logic of the market. But there is even more at stake here than the obliteration of public concerns, the death of the social, the emergence of a market-based fundamentalism that undercuts the ability of people to understand how to translate the privately experienced misery into collective action, and the elimination of the gains of the welfare state. There is also the growing threat of displacing "political sovereignty with the sovereignty of the market, as if the latter has a mind and morality of its own."[200]

As democracy becomes a burden under the reign of neoliberalism, civic discourse disappears and the reign of unfettered social Darwinism, with its survival-of-the-slickest philosophy, emerges as the template for a new form of proto-fascism. None of this will happen in the face of sufficient resistance, nor is the increasing move toward proto-fascism inevitable; but the conditions exist for democracy to lose all semblance of meaning in the United States. Against this encroaching form of fascism, a new language is needed for redefining the meaning of politics and the importance of public life.

Educators, parents, activists, workers, and others can address this challenge by building local and global alliances and engaging in struggles that acknowledge and transcend national boundaries, but also engage in modes of politics that connect with people's everyday lives. Democratic struggles cannot underplay the special responsibility of intellectuals to shatter the conventional wisdom and myths of neoliberalism with its stunted definition of freedom and its depoliticized and dehistoricized definition of its own alleged universality. As the late Pierre Bourdieu argued, any viable politics that challenges neoliberalism must refigure the role of the state in limiting the excesses of capital and providing important social provisions.[201]

Social movements must address the crucial issue of education as it develops throughout the cultural sphere because the "power of the dominant order is not just economic, but intellectual — lying in the realm of beliefs," and it is precisely within the domain of ideas that a sense of utopian possibility can be restored to the public realm.[202] Democracy necessitates forms of education that provide a new ethic of freedom and reassert collective identity as a central preoccupation of a vibrant democratic culture and society. Such a task, in part, suggests addressing the crucial pedagogical challenge of educating individuals and groups as social actors while refusing to allow them to be portrayed simply as victims.

Pondering the devastation following decades of European fascism, the theorist Theodor Adorno once wrote that "the premier demand upon all education is that Auschwitz not happen again."[203] While recognizing that the particularity of Auschwitz as a specific historical event should never be generalized, I believe that Adorno's comment extends beyond the reality of Auschwitz and speaks to the need to grasp the deeper meaning of education as a political and ethical intervention into what it means to shape the future. Every debate about education should address the important responsibility it has in preventing any relapse into barbarism from happening again. The time to act is now because the stakes have never been so high and the future so dark.

# Notes

1. George Monbiot, "States of War," *The Guardian/UK*, 14 October 2003. www.commondreams.org/views03/1014-09.htm
2. Jorge Mariscal, "'Lethal and Compassionate': The Militarization of US Culture," *CounterPunch*, 5 May 2003 www.counter punch.org/mariscal05052003.html
3. Kevin Baker, "We're in the Army Now: The G.O.P.'s Plan to Militarize Our Culture," *Harper's* (October 2003): 38.
4. Ibid., p. 37.
5. Ibid.
6. David Goodman, "Covertly Recruiting Kids," *Baltimore Sun*, 29 September 2003. www.commondreams.org/views03/1001-11.htm
7. Elissa Gootman, "Metal Detectors and Pep Rallies: Spirit Helps Tame a Bronx School," *New York Times*, 4 February 2004, p. C14.
8. Gail R. Chaddock, "Safe Schools at a Price," *Christian Science Monitor*, 25 August 1999, p. 15.
9. Tamar Lewin, "Raid at High School Leads to Racial Divide, Not Drugs," *New York Times*, 9 December 2003, p. A16.
10. Jeremy Brecher, "Globalization Today," in *Implicating Empire: Globalization and Resistance in the 21st Century World Order*, edited by Stanley Aronowitz and Heather Gautney (New York: Basic Books, 2003), p. 202.
11. Senator Robert C. Byrd, "Challenging 'Pre-emption'," *The Nation*, 15 December 2003. www.commondreams.org/views03/1215-12.htm
12. Thomas L. Friedman, "Crazier Than Thou," *New York Times*, 13 February 2002, p. A31.
13. Sheldon S. Wolin, "A Kind of Fascism Is Replacing Our Democracy," Long Island, NY, *Newsday*, 18 July 2003. www.commondreams.org/views03/0718-07.htm
14. Walter Cronkite, "The Trial of Saddam Hussein," DenverPost. com (21 December 2003). www.denverpost.com/Stories0,

141336~1839593,00.html. An extensive list of international agreements broken by the United States can be found in Rich Du Boff, "Mirror Mirror on the Wall, Who's the Biggest Rogue of All?" *ZNet Commentary*, 7 August 2003. Xnetupdates@ smail.zmag.org

15. Noam Chomsky, "There Is Good Reason to Fear Us," *Toronto Star*, 7 September 2003. www.commondreams.org/views03/0907-03.htm

16. Senator Robert C. Byrd, "Challenging 'Pre-emption'," *The Nation*, 15 December 2003. www.commondreams.org/views03/1215-12.htm

17. This policy is spelled out in great detail in Donald Kagan, Gary Schmitt, and Thomas Donnelly (principal author), *Rebuilding America's Defenses* (Washington, D.C.: Project for the New American Century, September 2000).

18. See Christopher Scheer, Lakshmi Chaudhry, and Robert Scheer David, *The Five Biggest Lies Bush Told Us About Iraq* (New York: Seven Stories Press, 2003); David Corn, *The Lies of George W. Bush* (New York: Crown, 2003).

19. Mark Trevelyn, "Bush Challenged on 'Safer America' Union Message," *Reuters News Service*, 21 January 2004. www.common dreams.org/cgi-bin/print.cgi?file=headlines04/0121-04.htm

20. Robert Jay Lifton, "American Apocalypse," *The Nation*, 22 December 2003, p. 12. These themes are developed extensively in Robert Jay Lifton, *Super Power Syndrome: America's Apocalyptic Confrontation with the World* (New York: Thunder Mouth Press, 2003).

21. Benjamin R. Barber, "Democracy Cannot Coexist with Bush's Failed Doctrine of Preventive War," *Los Angeles Times*, 3 December 2003. www.mail-archive.com/arafiyan@araf.net/msg01212.html. For a more extensive treatment of this issue by Barber, see Benjamin R. Barber, *Fear's Empire: War, Terrorism, and Democracy* (New York: Norton, 2003).

22. Graydon Carter, "The President? Go Figure," *Vanity Fair* (December 2003): 69. For an extensive analysis of the budget deficit, see Richard Kagan, "Deficit Picture Even Grimmer than New CBO Projections Suggest," *Center on Budget and Policy Priorities*, 26 August 2003. www.cbpp.org/8-26-03bud.htm

23. On the tax issue, see Paul Krugman, *Fuzzy Math: The Essential Guide to the Bush Tax Plan* (New York: Norton, 2001).

24. Larry Wheeler and Robert Benincase, "State Budget Belt-Tightening Squeezes Health Care for Kids," *USA Today*, 19 December 2003, p. 15A.

25. Center on Budget and Policy Priorities, "Up to 1.6 Million Low-Income People — Including About Half a Million Children — Are Losing Health Coverage Due to State Budget Cuts," 22 December 2003. www.cbpp.org/12-22-03health-pr.htm

26. Children's Defense Fund, "White House Wages Budget War Against Poor Children," Press release, 3 February 2003. www.cd factioncouncil.org/FY2004_pressrelease.htm

27. "Rep Bernie Sanders vs. Chairman Alan Greenspan," *Common Dreams News Center*, 16 July 2003. www.commondreams.org/views03/0716-13.htm

28. Cited in Bernie Sanders, "USA: Ex-Im Bank, Corporate Welfare at its Worst," *Corporate Watch*, 15 May 2002, p. 1. www.corpwatch.org/news/PND.jsp?articleid=2570

29. Jackson Lears, "How a War Became a Crusade," *New York Times*, 11 March 2003, p. A29.

30. President George W. Bush, Address to Joint Session of Congress, "September 11, 2001, Terrorist Attacks on the United States."

31. Gary Wills, "With God on His Side," *New York Times Sunday Magazine*, 30 March 2003, p. 29.

32. Ann Coulter, *Treason: Liberal Treachery from the Cold War to the War on Terrorism* (New York: Crown Forum, 2003), p. 16.

33. Coulter, cited in Jay Bookman, "Ann Coulter Wants to Execute You," *Atlanta Journal-Constitution*, 18 February 2002. www.indybay.org/news/20002/02/116560.php

34. Cited in Rich Cowan and Dalya Massachi, "Challenging the Campus Right," *The Public Eye*, 17 December 2003. www.publiceye.org/eyes/campus.html

35. Kathleen Parker, "Politics Are Out of Place in a Time of War," *Townhall*, 1 November 2003. www.townhall.com/columinists/Kathleenparker/kp20031101.shtml

36. Umberto Eco, "Eternal Fascism: Fourteen Ways of Looking at a Blackshirt," *New York Review of Books* (November-December 1995): 12.

37. Ibid.
38. Paul Krugman, "The Uncivil War," *New York Times*, 25 November 2003, p. A29.
39. For a brilliant analysis of the link between the Bush Administration's war on terrorism and the assault on constitutional freedoms, see David Cole, *Enemy Aliens: Double Standards and Constitutional Freedoms in the War on Terrorism* (New York: New Press, 2003).
40. Ben Bagdikian, "Beware the Geeks Bearing Lists," *ZNet Commentary*, 24 December 2002. www.Zmag.org/sustainers. content/2002-12/07bagdikian.cfm
41. Anthony Lewis, "Un-American Activities," *New York Review of Books*, 23 October 2003, p. 18.
42. This issue is taken up in great detail in Cynthia Brown, ed., *Lost Liberties: Ashcroft and the Assault on Personal Freedom* (New York: New Press, 2003); Nat Hentoff, *The War on the Bill of Rights and the Gathering Resistance* (New York: Seven Stories Press, 2003); and David Cole, *Enemy Aliens* (New York: New Press, 2003).
43. Arundhati Roy, *War Talk* (Boston: South End Press, 2003), p. 34.
44. Ryan J. Foley, "Feds Win Right to War Protesters' Records," *Miami Herald*, 7 February 2003. http://www.miami.com/mld/ miamiherald/news/breaking_news/7901637.htm
45. I want to thank my wonderful colleague, Sophia A. McClennen, for bringing this case to my attention.
46. Juan Stam, "Bush's Religious Language," *The Nation*, 22 December 2003, p. 27.
47. There are many excellent books dealing with the rise of right-wing authoritarianism in the United States. Some examples include: Charles Higham, *American Swastika* (New York: Doubleday, 1985); Susan Canedy, *America's Nazis* (Menlo Park, Calif.: Markgraf, 1990); Russ Bellant, *Old Nazis, The New Right, and the Republican Party* (Boston: South End Press, 1991); Paul Hainsworth, ed., *The Extreme Right in Europe and North America* (London: Pinter, 1992); Chip Berlet, Matthew Lyons, and Suzanne Phar, eds., *Eyes Right: Challenging the Right-Wing Backlash* (Boston: South End Press, 1995); Sara Diamond, *Roads to Domination: Right-Wing Movements and Political Power in the*

United States (New York: Guilford, 1995); Michael Novick, *White Lies, White Power* (Monroe, Maine: Common Courage Press, 1995); Lyman Tower Sargent, ed., *Extremism in America* (New York: New York University Press, 1995); Chip Berlet and Matthew Lyons, *Right-Wing Populism in America: Too Close for Comfort* (New York: Guilford, 2000); Martin A. Lee, *The Beast Reawakens: Fascism's Resurgence from Hitler's Spymasters to Today's Neo-Nazi Groups and Right-Wing Extremists* (New York: Routledge, 2000).

48. *Newsweek* Interview, "Nelson Mandela: The U.S.A. Is a Threat to World Peace," *Newsweek Web Exclusive*, 11 September 2002. www.msnbc.com/news/806174.asp?cp1=1

49. "European Majority Sees United States as Greatest Threat to World Security, Above Even North Korea," *Newsweek Web Exclusive*, 7 November 2003. www.intelmessages.org/messsages/National_Security/wwwboard/messages_03/6148

50. Nigel Morris, "Livingston Says Bush Is 'Greatest Threat to Life on Planet'," *The Independent/UK*, 18 November 2003. portland.indymedia.org/en/2003/11/275040.shtml

51. See, "George Soros Interview on NOW with Bill Moyers," 12 September 2003. Transcript available online: http://www.pbs.org/now/. Soros develops this position in greater detail in George Soros, *The Bubble of American Supremacy* (New York: Public Affairs, 2004).

52. This issue is discussed in Harvey Wasserman and Bob Fitrakis, "Senator Byrd, Major Media Spread Coverage of Bush-Nazi Nexus," *Free Press* (Columbus, Ohio), 22 October 2003. http://www.scoop.co.nz/mason/stories/HL0310/S00193.htm. On the same day that this story broke, the Associated Press ran a national story connecting President Bush's grandfather, Prescott Bush, to Adolf Hitler. Bush's grandfather, it appears, had his bank seized by the federal government because he had helped finance Adolf Hitler's rise to power.

53. Michael Lind, *Made in Texas: George W. Bush and the Southern Takeover of American Politics* (New York: Basic Books, 2002).

54. Zbigniew Brzezinski, "To Lead, US Must Give Up Paranoid Policies," *International Herald Tribune*, 15 November 2003. www.commondreams.org/headlines03/1115-01.htm

55. Rift Goldstein, "Cheney's Hawks 'Hijacking Policy',"
    *Commondreams*, 30 October 2003. www.commondreams.org/
    headlines03/1030-08.htm
56. Matthias Streitz, "US Nobel Laureate Slams Bush Gov't as
    'Worst' in American History," *Der Spiegel*, 29 July 2003. www.
    commondreams.org/headlines03/0729-06.htm
57. Arundhati Roy, "Instant-Mix Imperial Democracy (Buy One,
    Get One Free)," *Common Dreams*, 18 May 2003. www.
    commondreams.org/views03/0518-01.htm
58. Ibid.
59. Ibid.
60. Arundhati Roy, *War Talk* (Cambridge, Mass.: South End Press,
    2003), pp. 36-37. On the growing right-wing politicization of
    the United States Supreme Court, see Martin Garbus, *Courting
    Disaster: The Supreme Court and the Unmaking of American Law*
    (New York: Times Books, 2002).
61. See, "Testimony of Attorney General John Ashcroft to the
    Senate Committee on the Judiciary," 6 December 2001. www.
    usdoj.gov/ag/testimony/2001/
62. Roy has been lambasted in the conservative *Weekly Standard*,
    which gave her the facetious "Susan Sontag Award" for anti-war
    comments. The *New Republic* followed suit with its equally
    absurd "Idiocy Award." Roy responded to the increasing chorus
    of criticism with an article in the *Guardian*, in which she argued
    that the label of Anti-Americanism used against her simply
    meant that "the chances are that he or she will be judged before
    they're heard and the argument will be lost in the welter of
    bruised national pride." See, Arundhati Roy, "Not Again," *The
    Guardian*, 27 September 2002. www.ratical.org/ratville/CAH/
    AR092702.html
63. Wolin, cited in Alexander Stille, "The Latest Obscenity Has
    Seven Letters," *New York Times*, 13 September 2003, p. B17.
64. Sheldon Wolin, "Inverted Totalitarianism: How the Bush
    Regime is Effecting the Transformation to a Fascist-Like
    State," *The Nation*, 19 May 2003, p. 13.
65. Ibid., pp. 13-14.
66. Ibid., pp. 13-14.
67. Ibid., pp. 14-15.

68. James Traub, "Weimar Whiners," *New York Times Magazine*, 1 June 2003, p. 11.

69. David Cole, *No Equal Justice: Race and Class in the American Criminal Justice System* (New York: New Press, 1999); Christian Parenti, *Lockdown America: Police and Prisons in the Age of Crisis* (London: Verso, 1999); Marc Mauer, *Race to Incarcerate* (New York: New Press, 1999); Marc Mauer and Meda Chesney-Lind, *Invisible Punishment: The Collateral Consequences of Mass Imprisonment* (New York: New Press, 2002).

70. Pierre Tristam, "One Man's Clarity in America's Totalitarian Time Warp," *Daytona Beach News-Journal*, 27 January 2004. www.commondreams.org/views0401027-08.htm

71. Bertram Gross, *Friendly Fascism: The New Face of Power in America* (Montreal: Black Rose Books, 1985).

72. Umberto Eco, "Eternal Fascism: Fourteen Ways of Looking at a Blackshirt," *New York Review of Books* (November-December 1995): 15.

73. Kevin Passmore, *Fascism* (London: Oxford University Press, 2002), p. 90.

74. Ibid., p. 19.

75. Alexander Stille, "The Latest Obscenity Has Seven Letters," *New York Times*, 13 September 2003, p. 19.

76. Mark Neocleous, *Fascism* (Minneapolis: University of Minnesota Press, 1997), p. 91.

77. Bill Moyers, "This Is Your Story: The Progressive Story of America, Pass It On," Speech to the "Take Back America" Conference, 4 June 2003. www.utoronto.ca/csus/pm/moyers.htm

78. There has been a drastic increase in income and wealth inequality in the last few decades. For example, Paul Krugman, using data from the Congressional Budget Office, recently pointed out that "between 1973 and 2000 the average real income of the bottom 90 percent of American taxpayers actually fell by 7 percent. Meanwhile, the income of the top 1 percent rose by 148 percent, the income of the top 0.1 percent rose by 343 percent and the income of the top 0.01 percent rose 599 percent." Paul Krugman, "The Death of Horatio Alger," *The Nation*, 5 January 2004, p. 16.

79. William Greider, "The Right's Grand Ambition: Rolling Back the 20th Century," *The Nation*, 12 May 2003, pp. 1-12.

80. See, Jurgen Habermas, *The Structural Transformation of the Public Sphere*, reprint ed. (Cambridge: MIT Press, 1991); David Harvey, *Spaces of Capital: Towards a Critical Geography* (New York: Routledge, 2001). The literature on the politics of space is far too extensive to cite, but of special interests are Michael Keith and Steve Pile, eds., *Place and the Politics of Identity* (New York: Routledge, 1993); Doreen Massey, *Space, Place, and Gender* (Minneapolis: University of Minnesota, 1994), and Margaret Kohn, *Radical Space: Building the House of the People* (Ithaca: Cornell University Press, 2003).

81. Jo Ellen Green Kaiser, "A Politics of Time and Space," *Tikkun* 18, no. 6 (2003): 18-19.

82. Margaret Kohn, *Radical Space: Building the House of the People* (Ithaca: Cornell University Press, 2003), p. 7.

83. Jo Ellen Green Kaiser, "A Politics of Time and Space," pp. 17-18.

84. Zygmunt Bauman, *Globalization: The Human Consequences* (New York: Columbia University Press, 1998), pp. 25-26.

85. Susan Buck-Morss, *Thinking Past Terror* (New York: Verso, 2003), p. 29.

86. Stanley Aronowitz, *The Last Good Job in America* (Lanham, Md.: Rowman and Littlefield, 2001), p. 160.

87. Richard Falk, "Will the Empire Be Fascist?" *The Transnational Foundation for Peace and Future Research*, 24 March 2003. www.transnational.org/forum/meet/2003/Falk_FascistEmpire.html

88. Victoria de Grazia, *The Culture of Consent: Mass Organization of Leisure in Fascist Italy* (New York: Cambridge University Press, 2002) [original publication 1981].

89. Robert McChesney and John Nichols, *Our Media, Not Theirs: The Democratic Struggle Against Corporate Media* (New York: Seven Stories Press, 2002), pp. 48-49.

90. Jeff Sharlet, "Big World: How Clear Channel Programs America," *Harper's* (December 2003): 38-39.

91. On the relationship between democracy and the media, see Robert W. McChesney, *Rich Media, Poor Democracy: Communication Politics in Dubious Times* (New York: New Press, 1999).

92. Ibid., pp. 52-53.

93. Transcript of "NOW with Bill Moyers," 13 February 2004, p. 2.
94. Umberto Eco, "Eternal Fascism: Fourteen Ways of Looking at a Blackshirt," *New York Review of Books* (November-December 1995): 15.
95. Paul O'Neill, former U.S. Treasury Secretary who served in the Bush Administration for two years, claimed on the 11 January 2004 television program "60 Minutes" that Bush and his advisors started talking about invading Iraq 10 days after the inauguration, eight months before the tragic events of September 11. See CBS News, "Bush Sought Way to Invade Iraq," "60 Minutes" Transcript, 11 July 2004. www.cbsnews.com/stories/2004/01/09/60minutes/main592330.shtml. For a chronicle of lies coming out of the Bush Administration, see David Corn, *The Lies of George W. Bush* (New York: Crown, 2003).
96. Abbott Gleason, "The Hard Road to Fascism," *Boston Review* (Summer 2003). www.bostonreview.net/BR28.3/gleason.html
97. Bob Herbert, "Casualties at Home," *New York Times*, 27 March 2003, p. A27.
98. Renana Brooks, "The Language of Power, Fear, and Emptiness," *The Nation*, 24 June 2003. reclaimdemocracy.org/weekly-2003/bush-language-power- fear.html
99. The relevant excerpt from this interview can be found in "Millions and Millions Lost," *Harper's* (January 2004): 16.
100. This insight comes from Juan Stam, "Bush's Religious Language," *The Nation*, 22 December 2003, p. 27.
101. Bush's use of doublespeak is so pronounced that the National Council of Teachers of English awarded him its 2003 Doublespeak Award. See, www.govst.edu/users/ghrank/Introduction/bush2003.htm
102. Ruth Rosen, "Bush Doublespeak," *San Francisco Chronicle*, 14 July 2003. www.commondreams.org/views03/0714-10.htm. In January 2004, former Vice President Al Gore, in a major speech on Bush's environmental policies, said, "Indeed, they often use Orwellian language to disguise their true purposes. For example, a policy that opens national forests to destructive logging of old-growth trees is labeled Healthy Forest Initiative. A policy that vastly increases the amount of pollution that can be dumped into the air is called the Clear Skies

Initiative." Cited in Bob Herbert, "Masters of Deception," *New York Times*, 16 January 2004, p. A21.

103. Jennifer Lee, "U.S. Proposes Easing Rules on Emissions of Mercury," *New York Times*, 3 December 2003, p. A20.

104. Eric Pianin, "Clean Air Rules to Be Relaxed," *Washington Post*, 23 August 2003. www.washingtonpost.com/ac2/wp-dyn/A34334-2003Aug22?

105. The *New York Times* reported that the Environmental Protection Agency actually eliminated references to any studies that "concluded that warming is at least partly caused by rising concentrations of smokestack and tail pipe emissions and could threaten health and ecosystems." Cited in Huck Gutman, "On Science, War, and the Prevalence of Lies," *The Statesman*, 28 June 2003. www.commondreams.org/views03/0628-04.htm

106. For all of the direct government sources for these lies, see "One Thousand Reasons to Dump George Bush," especially the section titled "Honesty." thousandreasons.org/the_top_ten.html. Also see, David Corn, *The Lies of George W. Bush* (New York: Crown, 2003).

107. See David Corn, Ibid., pp. 228-30.

108. Both quotes can be found in Paul Krugman, "Standard Operating Procedure," *New York Times*, 3 June 2004, p. A17.

109. See Lloyd Grove, "Lowdown," *New York Daily News*, 11 January 2004. www.unknownnews.net/insanity011404.html

110. Cited in Paul Krugman, "Going for Broke," *New York Times*, 20 January 2004, p. A21.

111. Dana Milbank, "Religious Right Finds Its Center in Oval Office," *Washington Post*, 24 December 2001, p. A02.

112. Ibid.

113. Ibid.

114. Cited in Jill Lawrence, "Bush's Agenda Walks the Church-State Line," *USA Today*, 29 January 2003. www.usatoday.com/news/washington/2003-01-29-bush-religion_x.htm

115. See Stephen Mansfield, *The Faith of George W. Bush* (New York: Tarcher/Penguin, 2003). Cited in Sydney H. Schanberg, "The Widening Crusade," *Village Voice*, 15-21 October 2003. www.villagevoice.com.issues/0342/schanberg.phb

116. Robyn E. Blumner, "Religiosity as Social Policy," *St. Petersburg Times*, 28 September 2003. www.sptimes.com/2003/09/28/news_pf/Columns/religiosity_as_social.shtml

117. Cited in Paul Harris, "Bush Says God Chose Him to Lead His Nation," *The Guardian*, 1 November 2003. www.observer.co.uk. On the child tax credit, see, Bob Herbert, "The Reverse Robin Hood," *New York Times*, 2 June 2003, p. A17.

118. Joseph L. Conn, "Faith-Based Fiat," *Americans United for Separation of Church and State* (January 2002). www.au.org/churchstate/cs01031.htm

119. Robyn E. Blumner, "Religiosity as Social Policy," *St. Petersburg Times*, 28 September 2003. www.sptimes.com/2003/09/28/news_pf/Columns/religiosity_as_social.shtml

120. Jonathan Turley, "Raze the Church/State Wall? Heaven Help Us!" *Los Angeles Times*, 24 February 2003. www.enrongate.com/news/index.asp?id=169632

121. Alan Cooperman, "Paige's Remarks on Religion in Schools Decried," *Washington Post*, 9 April 2003. www.washingtonpost.com/wp-dyn/articles/A59692-2003Apr8.html

122. Robyn E. Blumner, "Religiosity as Social Policy."

123. Graydon Carter, "The President? Go Figure," *Vanity Fair* (December 2003): 70.

124. John Ashcroft, "Remarks to National Religious Broadcasters Convention in Nashville Tennessee on February 19, 2002." Text is distributed by the Department of State and is available online: usembassy-australia.state.gov/hyper/2002/0219/epf204.htm

125. Elizabeth Amon, "Name Withheld," *Harper's* (August 2003): 59.

126. Cited in William M. Arkin, "The Pentagon Unleashes a Holy Warrior," *Los Angeles Times*, 16 October 2003. www.latimes.com/news/opinion/commentary/la-oe-arkin16oct16,1,2598862,print.st

127. Ibid.

128. Cited in transcript from "NOW with Bill Moyers," 26 December 2003. www.pbs.org/now/transcript/transcript248_full.html

129. Gary Wills, "With God On His Side," *New York Times Sunday Magazine*, 30 March 2003, p. 26.

130. Cited in an interview with Reverend James Forbes Jr. on "NOW with Bill Moyers," 26 December 2003. www.pbs.org/now/transcript/transcript248_full.html

131. "Bill Moyers Interviews Union Theological Seminary's Joseph Hough," "NOW with Bill Moyers," 24 October 2003. www.commondreams.org/views03/1027-01

132. Heather Wokusch, "Make War Not Love: Abstinence, Aggression and the Bush White House," *Common Dreams News Center*, 23 October 2003. www.commondreams.org/views03/1026-01.htm

133. John R. Gillis, ed., *The Militarization of the Western World* (New Brunswick, N.J.: Rutgers University Press, 1989). On the militarization of urban space, see Mike Davis, *City of Quartz* (New York; Vintage, 1992); Kenneth Saltman and David Gabbard, eds., *Education as Enforcement: The Militarization and Corporatization of Schools* (New York: Routledge, 2003). For the current neo-conservative influence on militarizing American foreign policy, see Donald Kagen and Gary Schmidt, *Rebuilding America's Defenses*, which is one of many reports outlining such an issue, and developed under the auspices of The Project for the New American Century. Available online: www.newamericancentury.org

134. Michael S. Sherry, *In the Shadow of War: The United States Since the 1930s* (New Haven, Conn.: Yale University Press, 1995), p. xi.

135. Jorge Mariscal, "'Lethal and Compassionate': The Militarization of US Culture," *CounterPunch*, 5 May 2003. www.counterpunch.org/mariscal05052003.html

136. Ruth Rosen, "Politics of Fear," *San Francisco Chronicle*, 30 December 2003. www.commondreams.org/views02/1230-02.htm

137. Richard H. Kohn, "Using the Military at Home: Yesterday, Today, and Tomorrow," *Chicago Journal of International Law* 94 (Spring 2003): 174-75.

138. Ibid.

139. Sandra Rimer, "Unruly Students Facing Arrest, Not Detention," *New York Times*, 2 January 2004, p. 15.

140. Ibid.

141. Randall Beger, "Expansion of Police Power in the Public Schools and the Vanishing Rights of Students," *Social Justice* 29, nos. 1-2 (2002): 124.

142. Peter B. Kraska, "The Military-Criminal Justice Blur: An Introduction," in *Militarizing the American Criminal Justice System*, edited by Peter B. Kraska (Boston: Northeastern University Press, 2001), p. 3.

143. See, especially, Christian Parenti, *Lockdown America: Police and Prisons in the Age of Crisis* (London: Verso Press, 1999).

144. Kraska, "The Military-Criminal Justice Blur," p. 10.

145. Jonathan Simon, "Sacrificing Private Ryan: The Military Model and the New Penology," in *Militarizing the American Criminal Justice System*, edited by Peter B. Kraska (Boston: Northeastern University Press, 2001), p. 113.

146. These figures are taken from the following sources: Gary Delgado, "'Mo' Prisons Equals MO' Money," *Colorlines* (Winter 1999-2000): 18; Fox Butterfield, "Number in Prison Grows Despite Crime Reduction," *New York Times*, 10 August 2000, p. A10; Lewis, op. cit., p. A1.

147. Sanho Tree, "The War at Home," *Sojourner's Magazine* (May-June 2003): 5.

148. For some extensive analyses of the devastating effects the criminal justice system is having on black males, see Michael Tonry, *Malign Neglect: Race, Crime, and Punishment in America* (New York: Oxford University Press, 1995); Jerome Miller, *Search and Destroy: African-American Males in the Criminal Justice System* (Cambridge, Mass.: Cambridge University Press, 1996); David Cole, *No Equal Justice: Race and Class in the American Criminal Justice System* (New York: New Press, 1999); Christian Parenti, *Lockdown America: Police and Prisons in the Age of Crisis* (London: Verso, 1999); Marc Mauer, *Race to Incarcerate* (New York: New Press, 1999); Marc Mauer and Meda Chesney-Lind, *Invisible Punishment: The Collateral Consequences of Mass Imprisonment* (New York: New Press, 2002).

149. Cited in David Barsamian, "Interview with Angela Davis," *The Progressive* (February 2001): 35.

150. Ibid, p. 101.

151. Lisa Featherstone, "A Common Enemy: Students Fight Private Prisons," *Dissent* (Fall 2000): 78.
152. Carl Chery, "U.S. Army Targets Black Hip-Hop Fans." *The Wire/Daily Hip-Hop News*, 21 October 2003. www.sohh.com/article_print.php?content_ID=5162
153. Ibid.
154. David Garland, cited in Melange, "Men and Jewelry; Prison as Exile; Unifying Laughter and Darkness," *Chronicle of Higher Education*, 6 July 2001, p. B4.
155. Mariscal, "Lethal and Compassionate: The Militarization of US Culture."
156. Matt Slagle, "Military Recruits Video-Game Makers," *Chicago Tribune*, 8 October 2003, p. 4.
157. Nick Turse, "The Pentagon Invades Your Xbox," *Dissident Voice*, 15 December 2003. www.dissidentvoice.org/Articles9/Turse_Pentagon-Video-Games.htm
158. For a list of such "toys," see Nicholas Turse, "Have Yourself a Pentagon Xmas," *The Nation*, 5 January 2004, p. 8. For a more extensive list, visit www.tomdispatch.com
159. R. Lee Sullivan, "Firefight on Floppy Disk," *Forbes*, 20 May 1996, pp. 39-40.
160. Gloria Goodale, "Video Game Offers Young Recruits a Peek at Military Life," *Christian Science Monitor*, 31 May 2003, p. 18.
161. Wayne Woolley, "From 'An Army of One' to Army of Fun: Online Video Game Helps Build Ranks," *Times-Picayune*, 7 September 2003, p. 26.
162. This description comes from "Gaming News — October 2003" and is available at www.gamerstemple.com/news/1003/100331.asp
163. This quote comes from "Gaming News — October 2003" and is available at www.gamerstemple.com/news/1003/100331.asp
164. Nick Turse, "The Pentagon Invades Your Xbox," *Dissident Voice*, 15 December 2003. www.dissidentvoice.org/Articles9/Turse_Pentagon-Video-Games.htm
165. Maureen Tkacik, "Military Toys Spark Conflict on Home Front," *Wall Street Journal*, 31 March 2003, p. B1.

166. Amy C. Sims, "Just Child's Play," Fox News Channel, 21 August 2003. www.wmsa.net/news/FoxNews/fn-030822_childs_play.htm

167. Mike Conklin, "Selling War at Retail," *Chicago Tribune*, 1 May 2003, p. 1.

168. Both quotes are from Cathy Horyn, "Macho America Storms Europe's Runways," *New York Times*, 3 July 2003, p. A1.

169. Umberto Eco, "Eternal Fascism: Fourteen Ways of Looking at a Blackshirt," *New York Review of Books* (November-December 1995): 13.

170. This quote by Coulter has been cited extensively. It can be found at: www.coulterwatch.com/files/BW_2-003-bin_Coulter.pdf

171. Kevin Baker, "We're in the Army Now: The G.O.P.'s Plan to Militarize Our Culture," *Harper's* (October 2003): 38.

172. Susan George, "A Short History of Neo-Liberalism: Twenty Years of Elite Economics and Emerging Opportunities for Structural Change," *Global Policy Forum*, 24-26 March 1999. www.globalpolicy.org/globaliz/econ/histneol.htm

173. There are a number of important works on the politics of neoliberalism. I have found the following particularly useful: Pierre Bourdieu, *Acts of Resistance: Against the Tyranny of the Market* (New York: New Press, 1998); Pierre Bourdieu, "The Essence of Neoliberalism," *Le Monde Diplomatique* (December 1998), www.en.monde-diplomatique.fr/1998/12/08bourdieu; Zygmunt Bauman, *Work, Consumerism and the New Poor* (London: Polity, 1998); Noam Chomsky, *Profit Over People: Neoliberalism and the Global Order* (New York: Seven Stories Press, 1999); Jean Comaroff and John L. Comaroff, *Millennial Capitalism and the Culture of Neoliberalism* (Durham, N.C.: Duke University Press, 2000); Anatole Anton, Milton Fisk, and Nancy Holmstrom, eds., *Not for Sale: In Defense of Public Goods* (Boulder, Colo.: Westview, 2000); Alain Touraine, *Beyond Neoliberalism* (London: Polity Press, 2001); Colin Leys, *Market Driven Politics* (London: Verso, 2001); Randy Martin, *Financialization of Daily Life* (Philadelphia: Temple University Press, 2002); Ulrich Beck, *Individualization* (London: Sage, 2002); Doug Henwood, *After the New Economy* (New York:

New Press, 2003); Lisa Duggan, *The Twilight of Equality: Neo-liberalism, Cultural Politics, and the Attack on Democracy* (Boston: Beacon Press, 2003); Pierre Bourdieu, *Firing Back: Against the Tyranny of the Market 2*, trans. by Loic Wacquant (New York: New Press, 2003).

174. Minqi Li, "After Neoliberalism," *Monthly Review* (January 2003), p. 21. Professor Minqi Li provides an important sum-mary of neoliberal polices and their effects. "A neoliberal regime typically includes monetarist policies to lower inflation and maintain fiscal balance (often achieved by reducing public expenditures and raising the interest rate), 'flexible' labor mar-kets (meaning removing labor market regulations and cutting social welfare), trade and financial liberalization, and privati-zation. These policies are an attack by the global ruling elites (primarily finance capital of the leading capitalist states) on the working people of the world. Under neoliberal capitalism decades of social progress and developmental efforts have been reversed. Global inequality in income and wealth has reached unprecedented levels. In much of the world, working people have suffered pauperization. Entire countries have been reduced to misery."

175. For example, a United Nations' Human Development Report, states that "the world's richest 1 percent receive as much income as the poorest 57 percent. The income gap between the richest 20 percent and the poorest 20 percent in the world rose from 30:1 in 1960 to 60:1 in 1990, and to 74:1 in 1999, and is projected to reach 100:1 in 2015. In 1999-2000, 2.8 bil-lion people lived on less than $3 a day, 840 million were undernourished, 2.4 billion did not have access to any form of improved sanitation services, and one in every six children in the world of primary school age were not in school. About 50 percent of the global nonagricultural labor force is estimated to be either unemployed or underemployed." Cited in Minqi Li, "After Neoliberalism," *Monthly Review* (January 2003), p. 21.

176. George Steinmetz, "The State of Emergency and the Revival of American Imperialism: Toward an Authoritarian Post-Fordism," *Public Culture* 15 (Spring 2003): 337.

177. Ibid.

178. Barry Bluestone and Bennett Harrison, *The Deindustrialization of America: Plant Closings, Community Abandonment and the Dismantling of Basic Industry* (New York: Basic Books, 1982), p. 6.

179. Stanley Aronowitz, *How Class Works* (New Haven: Yale University Press, 2003), p. 21.

180. Ibid., p. 101.

181. Stanley Aronowitz, "Introduction," in Paulo Freire, *Pedagogy of Freedom* (Lanham, Md.: Rowman and Littlefield, 1998), p. 7.

182. Pierre Bourdieu, *Firing Back: Against the Tyranny of the Market 2*, p. 38.

183. Doug Henwood, *After the New Economy* (New York: New Press, 2003); Kevin Phillips, *Wealth and Democracy: A Political History of the American Rich* (New York: Broadway, 2003); Paul Krugman, *The Great Unraveling: Losing Our Way in the New Century* (New York: W.W. Norton, 2003).

184. Stanley Aronowitz, *How Class Works*, p. 102.

185. William Greider, "The Right's Grand Ambition: Rolling Back the 20th Century," *The Nation*, 12 May 2003, p. 8.

186. Edward S. Herman and Robert W. McChesney, *The Global Media: The New Missionaries of Global Capitalism* (Washington, D.C.: Cassell, 1997), p. 3.

187. I address this issue in Henry A. Giroux, *Public Spaces, Private Lives: Democracy Beyond 9/11* (Lanham, Md.: Rowman and Littlefield, 2003).

188. James Rule, "Markets, in Their Place," *Dissent* (Winter 1998): 31.

189. Zygmunt Bauman, *The Individualized Society* (London: Polity Press, 2001). p. 107.

190. Ibid.

191. Alan Bryman, *Disney and His Worlds* (New York: Routledge, 1995), p. 154.

192. Of course, there is widespread resistance to neoliberalism and its institutional enforcers, such as the WTO and IMF, among many intellectuals, students, and global justice movements; but this resistance rarely gets aired in the dominant media and,

if it does, it is often dismissed as irrelevant or tainted by
Marxist ideology.

193. George Soros, "The US Is Now in the Hands of a Group of
Extremists," *The Guardian/UK*, 26 January 2004. www.
commondreams.org/views04/0126-01.htm

194. Pierre Bourdieu, "The Essence of Neoliberalism," *Le Monde
Diplomatique* (December 1998), p. 4. www.en.monde-diplo
matique.fr/1998/12/08bourdieu

195. Paul Tolme, "Criminalizing the Homeless," *In These Times*, 14
April 2003, pp. 6-7.

196. Staff of Democracy Now, "Uncharitable Care: How Hospitals
Are Gouging and Even Arresting the Uninsured," *Common-
Dreams*, 8 January 2004. www.commondreams.org/head
lines04/0108-07.htm

197. John L. Comaroff and Jean Comaroff, "Millennial Capitalism:
First Thoughts on a Second Coming," *Public Culture* 12, no. 2
(2000): 305.

198. Herbert Marcuse, *Technology, War and Fascism: The Collected
Papers of Herbert Marcuse*, vol. 1, edited by Douglas Kellner
(New York: Routledge, 1998).

199. John and Jean Comaroff, "Millennial Capitalism: First
Thoughts on a Second Coming," p. 332.

200. Ibid.

201. Pierre Bourdieu, *Acts of Resistance: Against the Tyranny of the
Market* (New York: New Press, 1998).

202. Pierre Bourdieu and Gunter Grass, "The 'Progressive'
Restoration: A Franco-German Dialogue," *New Left Review* 14
(March-April, 2003): 66.

203. Theodor Adorno, "Education After Auschwitz," in Theodor
Adorno, *Critical Models: Interventions and Catchwords* (New
York: Columbia University Press, 1998), p. 191.

# About the Author

Henry A. Giroux holds the Global TV Network Chair in Communications at McMaster University in Canada. His most recent books include: *Breaking Into the Movies: Film and the Culture of Politics* (Basil Blackwell, 2002), *Public Spaces/ Private Lives: Democracy Beyond 9/11* (Rowman and Littlefield, 2001), *The Abandoned Generation: Democracy Beyond the Culture of Fear* (Palgrave, 2003), *Take Back Higher Education: Race, Youth, and the Crisis of Democracy in the Post Civil Rights Era*, co-authored with Susan Searls Giroux (Palgrave Macmillan, 2004) and his forthcoming book, *The Terror of Neoliberalism* (Paradigm, 2004). His primary research areas are: cultural studies, youth studies, critical pedagogy, popular culture, social theory, and the politics of higher education.